Instagram Marketing

A beginners guide to leveraging social media marketing, influencers, and advertising to grow your business!

© **Copyright 2019 - All rights reserved.**

The content contained within this book may not be reproduced, duplicated or transmitted without direct written permission from the author or the publisher.

Under no circumstances will any blame or legal responsibility be held against the publisher, or author, for any damages, reparation, or monetary loss due to the information contained within this book. Either directly or indirectly.

Legal Notice:
This book is copyright protected. This book is only for personal use. You cannot amend, distribute, sell, use, quote or paraphrase any part, or the content within this book, without the consent of the author or publisher.

Disclaimer Notice:
Please note the information contained within this document is for educational and entertainment purposes only. All effort has been executed to present accurate, up to date, and reliable, complete information. No warranties of any kind are declared or implied. Readers acknowledge that the author is not engaging in the rendering of legal, financial, medical or professional advice. The content within this book has been derived from various sources. Please consult a licensed professional before attempting any techniques outlined in this book.

By reading this document, the reader agrees that under no circumstances is the author responsible for any losses, direct or indirect, which are incurred as a result of the use of information contained within this document, including, but not limited to, — errors, omissions, or inaccuracies.

Table of Contents

Introduction 1
Chapter 1: What is Instagram Marketing? 2
    How to Post 3
    Picking a Theme 10
    Promoting Posts 11
    Going Live 12
    Sponsorship Opportunities 14
    Watch Your Analytics 18
Chapter 2: How You Can Use Instagram to Grow Your Business 20
    Link Your Website 21
    Provide a Form of Contact 22
    Avoid Hard Selling 23
    Meet Your Peers 24
    Track Growth 25
    Interact and Follow Back 26
    A Smart Business Plan 27
Chapter 3: Strategies for Growing Your Instagram Following 36
    Create a Call to Action 36
    Interact with Locals 38
    Follow Famous People 39
    Become a Part of a Conversation 40
    Create a Dedicated Hashtag 41
    Provide Results 43
    Monitor Tagged Photos 44
    Don't Disappear Without Warning 47
    Can You Purchase Followers? 48
Chapter 4: How to Run Ads on Instagram 53
    Customizing Your Ad 54
    Advertising on Stories 59
    Keeping Ads Intriguing 61
    How Often Should You Advertise? 64
    Comparative Advertising 65

Chapter 5: Influencer Marketing **70**
    Collaborations... 71
    Benefits of Influencer Marketing 76
    Things to Keep in Mind.. 80
    Rules and Regulations... 82
    Work Your Way Up 85
Chapter 6: Examples of Businesses That Have Used Instagram Marketing Effectively **87**
Chapter 7: Other Social Media Platforms to Use for Business Growth **108**
    Facebook 108
    Twitter... 111
    Tumblr... 113
    LinkedIn.. 116
    How Many Pages Should a Business Have? 118
Chapter 8: How to Keep Momentum Going **121**
    Spreading the Word 121
    Social Media Manager... 123
    Change Your Approach 124
    Dedicated Live Streams... 126
    Geotagging Locations.. 127
    Your Interactions... 128
Conclusion **131**

Introduction

Thank you for taking the time to read this book on Instagram marketing.

This book covers the topic of Instagram and will educate you on how this social media platform can be used to grow a large following, build a strong brand image, and increase your sales figures.

In the following chapters, you will learn about how the Instagram algorithm works, how to create content that will attract new customers, and how to use a variety of advertising methods to grow your business on Instagram.

Also included is a section covering the other social media platforms you might like to make use of when growing your business, and the features, pros, and cons of each.

At the completion of this book you will have a good understanding of how to use Instagram to your advantage and be armed with a variety of strategies to increase your following and sales alike.

Once again, thanks for choosing this book, I hope you find it to be helpful!

Chapter 1: What is Instagram Marketing?

Most of us see Instagram as a fun way to pass the time, a portal to visual scrapbooks shared by ourselves, our loved ones, and even complete strangers. It is a place for people to connect by sharing snippets of their life as it happens. You have the ability to choose what others see and when they see it. Editing tools give you the freedom to alter your content in order to make it aesthetically your own. While this is all true, Instagram is also a place where businesses can grow. Marketing your business or yourself on Instagram is a marketing method that has recently produced immense amounts of success for people. No matter what you do or what you promote, using Instagram for advertising purposes is a great way to gain a following and spread the word about your brand.

Currently, there are around 1-billion users on this social media platform. It makes sense to begin your marketing efforts in a place where there is already an audience to respond to your content. Aside from making posts to promote your products, there are advertising options for creating targeted posts in order to get noticed by specific groups of people. No matter your experience level with online marketing, Instagram makes it easy for anyone to participate. Creating an account is free and the advertising guidelines are pay-per-click, so you only use your budget after you've got the clicks!

How to Post

There are 2 main ways that you can share content with your audience: posts and stories. Making a post on Instagram means that you are either sharing a photo or a video to your account that is viewable all the time. The post won't go anywhere unless you decide to archive or delete it. The placement of your post on your friends' timelines depends upon the Instagram algorithm. Normally, posts that get more interaction are placed higher up on newsfeeds. For the posts that you see in your own newsfeed, the accounts that you interact with the most are normally boosted on your algorithm. So, the more that people interact with your content, the higher the likelihood of it being boosted on newsfeeds.

Alternatively, a story lasts for 24 hours (unless you decide to delete it sooner). When you post a story, you also have the option of sharing either a photo or a video. Instagram has a lot of other fun features for your stories such as polls, questions, and music sharing. When you post a story, your audience has to physically click on it in order to view it. This is the main difference between posting directly onto your account and posting a story. Many accounts choose to post important things on their account and more personal things to their story. This keeps your feed less cluttered with posts that are not relevant to what you are intending to market.

Many social media marketing experts agree that having a cohesive feed is going to gain you a bigger following than posting haphazardly will. When there is too much going on, people might get too overwhelmed to truly look through all of your content. It's important to be clear about what your brand stands for by only posting only things that are relevant to your message and image. Think about what you are posting to your account and whether or not it makes sense for the brand you would like to build. This is going to vary depending on what type of business you are trying to grow.

You will need to post frequently in order to keep your followers engaged, but not so much to the point where it feels like spam. If you are ever unsure about making a post, think about how you would personally react to it. Does it seem interesting? Is there too much information to read? This is a very important question to ask, because if you wouldn't stop to notice it, then it is likely that others are going to react the same way.

Captions

When you make a post, you have the ability to make a statement along with it. You can put anything in the caption, such as a description about the image itself, or even a funny quote. Think about what kind of caption makes sense for your brand. Also consider ways that you can use your caption to engage your audience. Some of the following methods are ways that businesses have found success utilizing captions:

- **Offer a Discount Code**: If you are using Instagram to advertise something that you are selling, you can offer your followers a discount for finding you on Instagram. This can be as simple as a 10% off offer for mentioning that they follow you, but it will entice people to continue following you in case of more opportunities like this in the future.

- **Give Insight**: People like hearing behind-the-scenes information. Be personable with your followers. If you are making a post, explain why you are posting and what it means to you. This can help you to come off as an approachable person rather than someone who only wishes to promote a product.

- **Utilize Humor**: Another way to make your post personable is by using humor in your caption. Most people use Instagram as a way to pass the time. Seeing something that is clever and witty will likely be eye-catching, and this is exactly what you want when you are trying to grow your following.

- **Ask a Question**: A super easy way to get comments on your posts is by asking questions in the captions. This is a way to ask for engagement without feeling like you are spamming your followers.

- **Write Drafts**: If you think of a good caption but you have nothing to post, save it. Rather than using a great caption on a post that doesn't really matter, you can place it into a draft folder for when you are ready to use it. This is also a great way to make sure that you have a caption ready when you need to make a quick post.

Stories work a little differently when it comes to captioning. You can add text to your stories and place it where you want it. This text appears as an overlay on your photo or video. There are also GIFs that you can use; moving photos stored in a library that Instagram provides for you. The options of what you can do to embellish your stories are endless. Just remember, try not to make them too busy. People are going to be more receptive to something that is to the point and organized rather than something that contains an overwhelming amount of texts and GIFs.

Hashtags

Hashtags are an important tool for finding what you want on Instagram. It is also a beneficial tool that you can utilize when marketing. When you post a hashtag on Instagram, it creates a link to your post. For example, if you sell clothing and you hashtag your posts with "#style," your post will come up when anyone browses the #style tag (as long as your profile is public). There is a hashtag for virtually anything that you can imagine. Adding hashtags to your post is easy, and by doing so, you might be able to expand your audience.

While there aren't really any rules when it comes to using hashtags, there is a certain etiquette to using them successfully. Try not to overload your captions with too many hashtags. Your followers probably aren't going to want to skim over 30 tags when they see your posts. Using about 4-5 at the most usually works best. For example, you could use #style, #fashion, #clothing, #clothes, and #outfit if you were advertising a clothing brand. This is to the point, and it also makes sense based on what the brand is.

Something that you should steer clear of is using misleading hashtags. You don't want to tag a clothing post with the #dogs hashtag. This just doesn't make sense, and it will probably annoy users. Hashtags are meant to keep Instagram organized and help people to find exactly what they are looking for.

You can also use hashtags on your stories, not only your posts. When you are posting them here, you might be able to get away with posting a few more than usual because the story will disappear in 24 hours. They work the same way as they do when you place them in a caption; traffic will be driven to your story when people view that particular tag.

Timing

The time that you decide to make a post on Instagram is very important. Because there are so many users in so many different time zones, you should take into consideration when you are choosing to upload your posts. If you're a local business, you wouldn't want to post at 2AM because most people in your surrounding area will be sleeping. Consider posting in the morning instead.

It is a wise decision to spend a week or two observing when your followers are most active. Post at a variety of times and take note of what time of day and what days of the week attract the most engagement. Weekends are usually a great time to post because a lot of people are free. Even if you have a great post that you can't wait to share, hold off until it's a good time to post! This can really help you to get the most out of every post you make and have as much interaction with your followers as possible.

If you are ever unsure about the timing of your post, imagine if you were the audience. Is this a time when you are normally working? Sleeping? Busy? Putting yourself in their shoes is an easy way to determine if you are making the right decision. This is something that will likely vary depending on who your main audience is. For example, if you're marketing a product that is geared toward a younger audience, making a post during school hours probably isn't the best idea.

Assistance

There are additional apps that you can download in order to assist you with your success on Instagram. If you get stuck thinking about captions, there are apps that can provide you with ideas. These apps will often include a database of caption ideas that are proven successful based on engagement from other users. Another thing that you can do is to pay attention to what your followers post as their captions. When you see one that catches your eye, take note. Being observant is a great way for you to stay on top of what is popular and what works to attract an audience.

There are also apps that are available to help you determine which hashtags are currently trending. If you aren't sure about which tags to use on your post, you can upload what you want to post onto one of these apps and the tags will be generated for you. Just like anything else that trends, this can change depending on what is currently popular. Using an app that tracks hashtags can help you stay on top of what is trending at all times.

Some apps also show you the most beneficial times to make a post on Instagram. You can input your information in order for the app to scan where your followers live and what their most active hours are. There are dozens of different apps made to help people market their business on Instagram, and more are being produced every week. Have a look in the app store and choose a few to try out for yourself!

Picking a Theme

Instagram is a visual app, and what you post relates to the vision that you are expressing. Some people do not consider what they post in such depth, but if Instagram is being used for marketing purposes, it is something that you do need to consider. Having a theme is going to keep you on track and going to make your feed look cohesive. For example, if you are trying to advertise your beachwear clothing line, posting pictures of the clothing with seaside backgrounds will make sense. This is a theme that you can follow. Of course, you can stick to the theme by using other creative methods. Doing so will make your page appear more professional as well.

Your theme can also involve a color scheme. Using colors that go well together is another way to create a nice theme. Posting photos that feature mainly reds and pinks for a month and then switching to photos with blues and greens is a way to transition between themes. The great part is that there are no rules when it comes to how you'd like to abide by your theme. Instagram allows your creative side to shine through if you want to utilize it.

The main point to focus on is that your theme should make sense to the product or service that you are selling. When you are planning your next post, ensure that it would make sense to you as an outside observer. Leave as much of the guesswork out as possible. People like it when content is direct and intriguing.

Too much mystery and vague explanations might cause your audience to stray.

Promoting Posts

When you get the hang of creating interesting posts that are consistent with your brand and theme, you can take an additional step to get noticed by users. Promoting your posts will boost them on the Instagram algorithm, showing the posts to extra users that might potentially be interested in your products. If you are serious about Instagram marketing, you will want to make sure that you sign up for a business account. This is an easy step to take and you can even switch your personal account over to one at the click of a button. Having a business account will allow you to promote posts; it will also show you analytics so that you can see how much traffic your account is getting.

It does cost money to promote a post, but you get to choose the budget. You can even select a $1-budget to start with. Instagram will provide you with options of who you would like the post to be promoted to. First, think about your target audience - how old are they? If you want to select an age range, you are able to do so before the promotion begins. You can also decide on what region you would like to focus on. If it only makes sense to advertise locally, you can set this parameter to a more selective area. Alternatively, you can create a broad spectrum of where you'd like your post to appear.

The promotion is pay per click, meaning you only need to pay out of your budget after your post has been clicked on. This will ensure that you're getting your money's worth out of the campaign. When your budget runs out, the promotion will end. If you'd like to run it for a certain amount of time, you can specify this when you are creating the campaign, and then Instagram will distribute the funds based on the time period.

Utilizing these boosts can create a large amount of traffic to your account. People who might not have ordinarily been exposed to your content will get the chance to see it and potentially become a customer. This type of advertising does take a certain amount of luck, as well as trial and error when testing different audiences. However, if you have a cohesive account, your posts should speak for themselves!

Going Live

Going live on Instagram is one of the most interactive features, and it is exactly what it sounds like; it provides you with the opportunity to stream a live video feed from your account to your followers. This is a free feature and it can be utilized in many different ways. If you are a business account trying to advertise a product, going live is a way to connect with your followers while showing them what you have to offer. Your viewers can react to what you are doing by commenting in a chat box that appears on the live screen. These streams pop up in the same area as Instagram stories. You can choose to save the livestream for 24 hours in a story when you are done, or you can end it and delete it without saving.

Letting your viewers see your personality and hear your voice in real time is an excellent way to connect. People are also naturally curious. If they see a brand which they follow going live, they're quite likely to click on the video. Much like the posts that you decide to share, make sure your live streams make sense to your brand. You wouldn't want to live stream a car ride when you are a business page trying to sell a product. Think about what kind of content will match with what you already post to your page.

You do not have to approach a live stream in a marketing type of way. Beware of making the approach seem too much like an extended ad. Instead, demonstrate the product in a way that seems natural and casual. Think about how you would tell a friend about what you are selling. When your followers see the product being used live, this might entice them to want to try it out for themselves. Again, this is all relative to what type of product you are trying to market.

Another great aspect of going live is that you get to interact with your followers in real time. They can react to what's going on in the livestream, and even ask questions. This allows you to develop a direct line of communication with your fans, answer their questions about your products, and build a trusting relationship with them.

As your followers get to know you, they will likely start to look forward to your livestreams. They can be awkward in the beginning, but even if a limited number of viewers join, you are still providing an outreach that you did not have to start off with. It does take a little bit of courage to put yourself out there in that way but try to have fun! Going live when you are enjoying yourself is going to send a much better message than a stiff video stream of you trying to convince people to buy what you are selling.

Sponsorship Opportunities

A large part of Instagram marketing comes from sponsored posts. These posts are "sponsored" by collaborators that agree to work with you in order to create a mutually beneficial partnership. For example, a brand might decide to make a post featuring you that shows you using their product. This can work out great for accounts that are looking to expand their following. Users will be directed to your page after they see the brand post you. To get sponsored, you usually don't need to have an exceptionally large number of followers; that is a misconception. What brands look for is an account that stays consistent with quality content and has good levels of engagement on their posts. If you are already practicing the steps that we discussed earlier, then you are likely in the group of accounts that are considered marketable.

Another way that sponsored posts work is by having a brand send you their product, either for free or at a discounted price, in order for you to make a post that mentions them. This is a great way to show other brands that you are ready for sponsorship opportunities. The more brands that get to know you, the more you will build up your reputation in the industry. As mentioned, this type of opportunity is widely available to many users.

As your reputation builds, brands will start to come to you. Instead of drafting out messages to potential brands, your inbox will be full of offers. Some might even offer to pay you to work together! Those with larger followings and a track record of producing results on sponsorship deals have a greater chance of getting paid.

When you are just starting out, you are likely going to have to seek out the opportunities yourself. Think about this process like you're going on several job interviews. Remember, it might take a lot of declinations before you get your "yes" response. By putting yourself out there, you truly don't have anything to lose. You are allowing your account to be seen by larger brands that might not have noticed you in the first place. Sending a direct message is a good starting point for opening up some opportunities. Plan a draft of what you would like to say before you send your DM. You can consider including the following:

- **Explain Your Vision**: The brand needs to know what you are all about. Let them know about your mission, and remember, you are trying to sell your own brand. Don't only go into detail about what you *want* to do, but also, *how* you are going to accomplish it.

- **Remain Flexible**: Large brands want people that are easy to work with. Make sure that you remain professional, yet reasonable. If you do not think the offer is fair, simply turn it down and move onto the next option. Bad mouthing brands will only damage your reputation and make you appear unprofessional.

- **Make an Offer**: Instead of waiting for them to offer you something, propose your idea instead. This shows that you are serious about working together and that you have initiative. The worst thing that can happen is that you will be declined, but again, this is not an opportunity that was certain anyway. Keep your head up and try again.

- **Believe in the Brand**: If you decide to collaborate with a brand that does not share some of the same values or visions, it is going to show. Try to remain genuine with the sponsorship opportunities that you choose. Your followers aren't going to want to hear about a brand that makes no sense to your own message. It is always best to stay true to who you are.

Once you get an offer, you must read the contract carefully. Not every brand requires one, but a lot of them do. Make sure that you fully understand what is expected of you. Ensure that you are able to produce the content in the timeframe that is given. Some brands will give you deadlines, and if you do not meet them, you will not get paid or your pay can be deducted. Unfortunately, scams do exist. Some "brands" might be posing as successful companies that are simply looking to con users with the promise of exposure.

Try to do some research when you are presented with an opportunity. Take a look at the accounts of some other users who have worked with the brand. You can even take the time to DM a few of them to get a real review of how it went. The more that you can do to protect yourself, the safer you will be on Instagram. Those who fall privy to scams easily probably won't make it very far. It only takes some light research and common sense to avoid these problematic accounts.

All of the above strategies are great if you're building a personal brand and want to become an influencer. On the other hand, if you're building a company that is selling products of its own, then you can use this same kind of marketing to gain more exposure. Instead of approaching brands and offering to promote their products, you can approach influencers and micro-influencers on Instagram that are congruent with your brand and see if they'd be interested in promoting your products for you! Depending on the size of their following and the engagement they receive, you could offer them discounted products, free products, or even pay them to make a post promoting you. The use of influencers is one of the best and most affordable ways to rapidly grow your following on Instagram.

Watch Your Analytics

Having a business page allows you the opportunity to view your analytics. These figures show how many visitors you get to your page, how many times they click on certain links, and when they are most active. A benefit to having a business account over a personal one is that you are able to see a lot more of the behind the scenes statistics. Pay attention to which posts do well and try to determine a common denominator. It might be the content, but it also might be the time that you post.

Getting into the habit of regularly tracking these figures is going to get you far on Instagram. The tools are free and very easy to use. Most of the numbers appear at the click of a button. If you notice that your followers enjoy beach photos on weekday afternoons, you might want to consider making a promoted post that follows these guidelines.

Depending on your audience, you will begin to learn what works and what is most responded to. Analytics can also tell you how many of your new followers came from looking at a post, browsing a hashtag, and randomly discovering. This will help you determine if what you are posting is working. If you notice that your hashtags aren't effectively drawing people in, you might have to consider using some new ones. Make checking your analytics a daily habit, and you will soon learn how to get much more out of your posts.

Chapter 2: How You Can Use Instagram to Grow Your Business

Many businesses small and large alike are turning to Instagram in hopes of growing their brands. No matter what you do or sell, Instagram probably already has a community of people interested in it. If you can find a community on Instagram that are interested in what you have to say, you will find success. Instagram is great for getting the word out about a brand; it is also perfect for getting to know your customers. Brands who take the time and effort to be personable are the kind that see success on Instagram.

Instagram is no longer only for people to share experiences and events. It has actually become quite a large hub for buying and selling. Since millions of people use Instagram daily, the opportunities that you will encounter to grow your client base are practically endless. An important thing to remember is that success on social media can involve a little bit of luck. Having a post go viral can be huge for a brand's growth, but it's very hard to plan for this kind of event. However, if you're consistent with your efforts, your chances of finding success on Instagram will increase dramatically. If you can spend some time each day putting in the effort, you will begin to see results.

Link Your Website

A simple, but sometimes overlooked, first step is to link your company's website on your Instagram profile. While Instagram is great for making posts that show snippets of content, you still need to make sure that you have an effective and functional website that people can visit. This is especially true if you are selling a product. Customers cannot buy products directly from Instagram. A third-party website is needed in order to complete sales. Even if this is not your own website that you developed, it is necessary to have a place where customers can be redirected when they are ready to make a purchase.

Before you post a link to your website, make sure that there are no broken links or aspects of the site that only load halfway. Small details like this can make your website hard to browse and will often push customers away. Try not to overload the user with too much content; mention what is essential. Your website should answer questions before they are asked.

Once you have everything to your liking, visit your website from both a phone and tablet. Remember, each website will look different on the computer versus a mobile device. You will need to make sure that each version is formatted correctly. Since Instagram is a phone app, most users will be looking at your website from a mobile device, so make sure the site looks good when viewed on a phone.

Having a good website does not mean that you must spend a lot of money on it. This is a misconception that business owners often have. Especially if your business is new, make sure that your website gets traffic and that customers are actually interested in your products before investing too much money into a fancy website. It is much better to have a simple and functional website than an overloaded page that is difficult to navigate. Whether you are creating it yourself or hiring someone to create it for you, the functionality of your website is what should always come first.

Provide a Form of Contact

While Instagram DMs are a valid way to communicate, it helps to provide your customers with a more direct and professional way to talk to you. Make sure that you include your work phone number on your profile, or at least your work email address. When you run a business, it is important to give your clients an outlet for any questions or concerns. Being able to reach someone directly builds trust and builds your customer service reputation.

Aside from monitoring your phone and emails, it is also important to pay attention to what is said to you on Instagram. There are some people who prefer more informal communication, and that is exactly what social media provides. As mentioned, direct messages can be a quick and effective way for your clients to communicate with you. Make sure that you check them often and try to reply in a timely manner.

It is also wise to pay attention to the comments you receive. You might notice some helpful patterns that will make your marketing experience easier. Many people enjoy giving feedback on the app for the same reason of informality. You'll be able to see what your clients are enjoying and what you could improve on. Taking a poll every once in a while, is also a smart way to gain valuable insight into your customers preferences.

Avoid Hard Selling

Nobody wants to get on Instagram and see a bunch of posts persuading them to purchase things. This gets repetitive and old. You need to use your creativity when you are a business on Instagram; make customers interested in your products without forcing them to buy them. You will want to create a genuine interest in what you have to offer before you make any suggestions about buying it. Show or explain why your product is useful. This is where you can really unleash your creativity. What you post should be a direct reflection of what you have to offer your audience.

Avoid any spam-like interactions via DMs as well. A lot of companies make the mistake of sending mass messages to their followers. Most people will see this and instantly delete the message, and possibly block your page. If you are considering doing some client outreach, try to create a unique message that is down to earth and friendly in its approach. Try to start a conversation without putting the pressure of selling on top of it. By getting to know your customers, you will be able to grow in a more natural and effortless way.

Your aim should be to help your customers, not to persuade them into buying things that they don't need. Remember, people browse Instagram for fun. The environment is naturally going to be laid back. Showing people how your product fits into their lifestyle is going to be a much more effective selling strategy. Once you get a good handful of customers, the product should speak for itself.

Meet Your Peers

You know enough about Instagram marketing by now to know that it is essential to learn about your customers. This concept does not stop at potential clients. Consider getting to know your competition or other businesses that are of the same size. Introduce yourself to your peers, because you never know when you might be able to form a business relationship. This is also a way to establish a reputation. Try to branch out in all ways possible, and don't be afraid to be the first business to reach out.

It might seem like a weird concept, but it is a part of owning your own business. You need to be able to talk to other people, and this includes other business owners. Being successful in your given industry requires you to make a name for yourself. Show those other businesses that you know what you are doing, and make it clear what your intentions are. This approach should never be hostile, as developing a relationship with other businesses in your industry can often prove beneficial for both parties.

Sometimes, you can even establish a referral agreement with your competitors. By sending clients back and forth to one another, it gives you both the chance to grow. Becoming successful on Instagram has everything to do with other people. If you aren't doing your part, you shouldn't expect to gain any followers. This process will involve lot of trial and error. Not everyone is going to see your vision, and that is okay.

Track Growth

By using the tools that Instagram provides, and maybe some of your own, you can always keep track of how many followers you are gaining or losing. If you notice a spike in activity, take note of what action caused that result. This is a simple thing to do that only takes a little bit of time each day. By keeping track of your progress, you are also going to be able to compare your growth over longer periods of time. The success that you notice from month to month can be a great motivating factor.

When you are tracking your growth, you can also make a note of certain followers that you see a lot of interaction from. These will be your most loyal followers, the ones who always interact with what you post. It is important to have a group of people like this, even if it is a small group to start out with. Really try your best to establish great relationships with them because it will benefit you as your brand begins to grow. These people are the ones that are most likely to tell family and friends about your products and great customer service. They can also serve as great customer testimonials down the line.

Interact and Follow Back

When dealing with interactions on Instagram, know that they work both ways. If you have people who regularly interact with your content, it could be a good idea to return the favor. What makes the app so fun is that you have an opportunity to meet people from different backgrounds and different locations around the world. Keeping lines of communication open will help you be a more approachable brand. Show your followers the same engagement that you hope for on your own page. This can come in the form of likes or comments. If you feel compelled, you can also send some DMs expressing your opinions on their content.

Following back is an easy way to encourage people to stay following you. While there are no guarantees, if you share a mutual decision to follow, the other person can also feel valued. There are communities on Instagram that are dedicated solely for the purpose of following back. You can search through different follow back hashtags if you want to find some accounts like this. People create "follow trains" so that anyone who wants to obtain a following can continue to grow. The trains are meant to provide support to one another along the way.

Anyone can choose to participate in these trains, even brands. As long as you follow the rules of following back those who follow you, your audience will begin to grow. While this method isn't a way to guarantee sales, it is a way to expand your target audience. Having a larger following also gives your brand a level of credibility, and social proof, making it easier for your following to grow further.

A Smart Business Plan

Once you are familiar with the platform and what it takes to run a successful account, making a business plan should be the next step. This plan should be focused on how you can use Instagram in the most beneficial way for your business. A business plan is going to vary depending on what it is that you actually do or are trying to sell. Some businesses revolve around selling products, others around selling services. There are also businesses that prioritize selling a personal brand (known as an "influencer"). Once the research is done, it is time to decide what your business actually stands for and what you wish to accomplish.

Put it in Writing

For the benefit of yourself and your audience, express your mission statement in writing. Since this is social media, the description does not have to be extremely formal. If your business revolves around being approachable and current, you might want to throw in some humor and slang. No matter how you express it, just make sure that it makes sense. Tell the audience what you are all about and stick to that statement. Consistency is what will build up your reputation the fastest. This will also encourage customers to tell their friends and family about you.

Draft out some sentences on what your business is all about. Take a good look at the flow of the description and make sure that it accurately represents yourself and your brand. From there, you will be able to perfect it until it is ready. Next, put this statement somewhere on your profile and your website.

You want to answer the question that is on everybody's mind before it is asked: why do you sell the product or service that you do? There are countless clothing brands out there, but you will likely notice the one that advertises its eco-friendly stance because it stands out. That is what you need to aim for on Instagram; a detail that differentiates you from the rest. Be careful that you do not exaggerate your point too much. People turn away from the mundane just as fast as they do repetition.

Keep Track of Your Numbers

Part of owning a business has to do with monitoring all aspects of growth. Start by keeping a record of your sales. If your website does not already do this for you, keeping track manually isn't a bad idea. In the beginning, it shouldn't be too difficult to record your numbers and look back on them for reference. As your business grows, there is software that you can utilize that will keep track of this for you. Tracking sales isn't a way to boast or get ahead of yourself; it is the opposite. Knowing how much output is coming from your input is going to help you grow more.

If you are putting on sales every week but not experiencing much growth, this is probably an indication that you need to switch up your strategy. Try to create personal sales goals to reach that will keep you motivated and on track.

As mentioned earlier, it is also wise to keep track of your audience growth via Instagram analytics. Knowing what you are doing that attracts these spikes in numbers is going to help you. If you notice that going live and doing demonstrations of your product earns you followers and sales, then you can keep incorporating this strategy into your business plan. While Instagram is a fun way to share just about anything, it can also be a powerful business tool if used correctly.

Make Sure Everyone is on the Same Page

Keeping your brand consistent is important, as you already know. If you have employees working for you, you will need to make sure that they display the same values as you do when operating the company's Instagram page. In order for you to enforce your mission statement to your audience, everyone involved in the business must also be on board. This is a simple, yet often overlooked, standard to maintain. Those businesses who simply hire people to fill seats don't come off as cohesive. Your audience will be able to sense this when interacting with your page.

A strong team is going to provide you with strong results. Even if the business is your own and you only plan on hiring one person to assist you with social media, try to select someone with values that align with your own. These business decisions that you make early on have the ability to shape the entire future of your company. If a client has a bad interaction, there is a risk that you will not only lose out on a sale but also be the recipient of a bad review. Word can travel fast on Instagram.

Master Financial Planning

Once you get a little bit of momentum and your sales figures start to rise, you can consider expanding your business to encourage more growth. Think about some of the followings things that you can do when you begin earning more money:

- **Obtain New Products**: With some money to spend, you will be able to provide new products to your customers. If you decide to allocate some of your budget toward this goal, consider what your current customers have been most responsive to. This is where paying attention to analytics is going to come in handy. Based on Instagram's tools and your sales receipts, you will be able to see what type of products are the most sought after.

- **Update Visuals**: Another thing that you can consider doing with some of your spending money is hiring a professional photographer or graphic designer. Because Instagram is based on visuals, having quality images is something that can set you apart from the rest. If you do not have a professional camera, hiring someone to take photos that you can post on your Instagram and website might result in a boost in sales.

- **Give Back**: If it is in your mission to do kind things for the community, you can use some of your proceeds to give back. A lot of brands partner with charities, explaining that a certain portion of all sales will go to a charity of choice. People who believe in the mission of this charity might decide to support you on this reason alone. This is why it is important to speak up about the causes that you believe in.

- **Save Up**: Just because you have the additional money to spend on your business does not mean that you have to spend it right at this moment. Saving money is never a bad idea; it can provide you with a cushion in case of a slow sales period. Practicing this type of financial willpower is what makes for a great business operation.

- **Run Promotions**: As you should be familiar with by now, Instagram ads are a great way to give your business an extra boost. If you find yourself with a little bit of extra money in the budget, you can choose some of your most successful posts to promote. This is a quick and controlled way to make sure that people are seeing your posts.

Scan the Market

Your research doesn't end once you launch your Instagram page. Continuous research should be done in order to stay ahead of the trends. Social media platforms are places where certain things can go "viral." This is when something reaches popularity in a short amount of time. While you do not need to aim for your own posts to go viral, as this requires a lot of luck, you can always stay on top of what is relevant to the community.

There isn't a tool or a service that can really tell you what is popular. Simply by using Instagram on a regular basis, you will begin to see patterns of things that are currently popular. If it fits within your own brand, try to market some of your posts toward these trends. If people are being responsive to a certain format, it only makes sense to try out the same format for your own business.

Remember, try not to conform too much. People will notice when your interaction is not genuine or true to your own brand. It is a tricky balance that solely exists on this type of new-age social media marketing platform. There is a need for unique brands, yet they still need to be marketable. This is not to say that you should simply conform to what is currently successful, but you can adapt the things that make others successful to fit your own brand.

Listen to What the People Want

Checking in with your followers from time to time can provide you with some insight on what they expect from your company. Getting suggestions from those who will be purchasing your products is a great idea. Instagram allows you the option to hold polls that your followers can vote on. This is a great, informal way to learn about what your clients are most receptive to. For example, if you are a company that sells t-shirts, you can create a poll regarding t-shirt designs. This is also a way to encourage your followers to be interactive with your page.

Instagram makes it easy for your audience to contact you. Sending an Instagram DM can seem easier than calling or emailing a company. While all are valid forms of communication, you should make sure that you are paying attention to your Instagram DMs. People might offer suggestions or ask questions regarding your brand. It is an easy way for you to connect with your clients without coming across in a sales-like manner.

If you are just starting out on Instagram and no one is providing you with suggestions yet, take a look at what people are asking of similar brands. This is why scanning the market regularly is important. You can have the chance to get ahead of your competition by simply paying attention. This type of attention to detail makes for a successful company.

Perform Regular Maintenance

Trends on Instagram can change quickly from one day to the next. Staying relevant and interesting to your audience can take a good bit of trial and error. When you find something that works for you, stick with it, but not for too long. Posts that are successful are likely this way because they are relevant to what is currently happening. If you notice that people are being less responsive to your posts, it could be time to try something new. Even something as slight as a change in your caption style could be enough to revamp your content.

Maybe a visual change is what you need. Remember that having a theme on Instagram is an important step to coming across as cohesive. Consider changing your theme for the sake of updating your content. The changes don't have to be dramatic, but your audience will take notice and appreciate the little things that you do choose to upgrade. Make sure that you are also doing the same thing for your website.

Chapter 3: Strategies for Growing Your Instagram Following

Gaining followers on Instagram can be a challenge when you're first starting out on the platform. Luckily, there are plenty of ways that you can attract an audience and encourage others to follow you. The rate at which your following grows can sometimes involve a little bit of luck, but if you're proactive, you should see your numbers increasing consistently. In this chapter we'll cover some of the best ways to grow your Instagram following.

Create a Call to Action

In any form of marketing, creating a call to action is a smart strategy that is widely used by all types of businesses. A call to action is basically a tactic to create a response. This does not mean that you have to be deceptive toward your followers, but you must say something that will intrigue them and encourage interaction. Playing on enthusiasm is a great way to entice someone to react. You can mention an exciting upcoming event and ask your followers if they are excited too.

Excitement is one of the easiest emotions to act on. When people feel excited about something, they are more likely to respond in a positive way. Some companies decide to play on the opposite end of the spectrum and play on negative emotions: worry and sadness. An example of this type of call to action is a commercial urging you to donate money to neglected animals. This kind of content makes you feel bad which then encourages you to support the cause.

Another approach is the neutral approach. You can do this by asking a direct question in your caption. This will show your audience that you are expecting a response, but without the added pressure of making a purchase. This type of call to action seems to do really well on social media. Everyone wants to be included in the conversation, and this type of question gives them a chance to do so. You'll notice that some of the most popular accounts ask their followers basic questions in every caption, even if it doesn't have much to do with the content. When the interaction numbers on a post are higher, the more likely it will be boosted in the algorithm. As you can see, this is why interaction matters so much.

A lot of thought should go into your call to action. You must determine what your end goal is. In the case of gaining more followers, you will need to say something that will cause people to want to stick around. Asking about favorite movies probably won't cut it in this case. Perhaps you can ask a question about being excited for Summer; this can then transition into you mentioning that you have products that are great to use in the summertime. Small details like this will make a difference in your follower count.

It might seem taboo, but you are allowed to ask people to follow you. As direct as it sounds, sometimes when people see this written down, it triggers something. A direct reminder to hit the follow button might be all it takes to grow your audience. Don't forget to tell them *why* they should follow you. Of course, this doesn't necessarily mean that you should be messaging people to say this. Expressing it in a caption can be even more effective, while feeling less invasive.

Saying "don't forget" and adding something to look forward to is a great call to action that is appropriate for social media. You need to give your audience something to look forward to as you are making the suggestion. Imagine if someone were telling you to follow a page. You would probably want to know what was so special about it or what it stood for before you decided to follow. Putting yourself in the position of the customer can give you some ideas of ways to entice people to stick around.

Interact with Locals

Even though ecommerce businesses are normally not focused on a specific location, it could be a good idea to focus on your local audience when you're first trying to grow your following. Becoming a staple in your local scene is a good idea if you want to become a main competitor in your field. Those who try to gain followers from all over the world often come to realize that the follow is fleeting. A lot of people will follow you so that you follow back and then immediately unfollow you. That's not to say that this won't happen locally, but if you have a specific group in mind, you might be able to relate to them better.

Post content that is relevant to your local area. Tag some other local companies and encourage them to check out your posts. Trying to get featured on a relevant local page is also a great way to earn a following that is familiar with your area. If you have a physical location, posting pictures taken there can show people that you are centrally located.

Mention your Instagram page in person, too. If you interact with your clients on a regular basis, don't forget to mention that your company is on Instagram. This is something that can be said in passing and offered as a suggestion. Mentioning this on a regular basis to clients that you interact with will earn you a following made up of people who are genuinely interested in what you are selling. Seek out genuine people who are truly supportive of your business.

Follow Famous People

It sounds bizarre but following those who are famous can give you a boost in the follower count department. Celebrities often have millions of followers. You can look for the small blue "verified" check marks on profiles to determine if someone is recognized as a famous user. This mark indicates that this person is real and not being impersonated. Getting the check mark is a process, and not everyone who applies will be accepted. This is how you can determine the authenticity of those profiles that garner a lot of attention.

Following popular accounts isn't all that it takes to grow your own audience; you will have to interact. Take a small bit of time each day to make sure that you are engaging with some big accounts. Leave comments that are relevant so that the larger audience can see you. All it takes is a "viral" comment that will lead to people exploring your page. Curiosity takes over a lot of the time on Instagram, so be prepared for those curious onlookers that might transfer over into followers.

Liking and agreeing with comments that other users post on popular pages can create the same type of ripple effect that leads to popularity. People like to form alliances, and as long as you aren't hurting anyone's reputation, it is okay for you to participate in these conversations in the comments section of Instagram.

Become a Part of a Conversation

To elaborate a bit more, talking in threads to other users is going to get you noticed. You don't necessarily have to join a conversation that is on a notable user's page; you can also jump in when you feel so inclined, no matter who is speaking. The great part about Instagram is that it is a place where you will probably see many different opinions expressed. Become a part of the conversation when you feel that you have something relevant to say on the topic.

A lot of business owners feel that it isn't right to talk to others while they are posting from a business page – the exact opposite is true, though. Being a relatable and down to earth business is going to be much better for your follower count. It will also show users that your page is being run by an actual person with a personality. Most businesses that go "viral" on Instagram can attribute at least some of their success to being interactive.

Create a Dedicated Hashtag

While you are familiar with the use of hashtags, sticking with ones that are popular isn't the only way to use them successfully. A hashtag can be anything that you want it to be. Creating your own can be great for your business. Many companies decide to create their own in order to stay on top of trends. People will know that your hashtag can be used to tag all things that are relevant to your business. From photos with your products to reviews about them, giving your customers this opportunity can encourage them to post about your brand.

Make sure that what you create isn't too long and hard to read. This is a mistake that will cause you to wonder why the hashtag isn't catching on. Nobody wants to spend time deciphering what your tag means. Using your company's name can be a starting point for creating your dedicated tag. No matter what you post, make sure that you include your own hashtag as well as the popular ones that you choose to utilize. Getting into this habit might encourage your followers to use the tag too when they are posting about your products.

You can include this hashtag into your other promotional marketing materials, too. This can be mentioned on your company website, flyers, signage, and even in your physical location. Spreading the word is going to be the main way for its use to catch on. When you use the tag, you are leading by example. Whenever someone clicks on the tag to browse it, posts that are relevant to you your business and your products will be found. It is an easy way for people to find exactly what they are looking for and it can help you out when you are more popular in the future.

Think of a catchy, short slogan that you can turn into a hashtag. Sometimes, a business name isn't enough to catch on. You will need to stand out from the crowd, and a catchy saying might be enough to do the trick. Think "I'm loving it" from McDonald's. Upon hearing the phrase, you probably knew exactly what company was being mentioned. This is the exact goal you should be trying to accomplish by creating a hashtag for your own business.

Provide Results

If your product comes with the promise of a lasting result, showing that result obtained by customers is a great thing that you can do to promote your product. For example, if you sell a dietary supplement, get your customers to send in before and after photos. Seeing real results is the best way that you can advertise a product; they will speak for themselves. While it is easy to tell customers about the product from a business standpoint, there is just something that is more relatable when the testimonial comes from someone who isn't going to financially benefit from promoting the product.

This type of marketing technique does not only apply to one type of product. You can show "results" with just about anything, even the way that clothing looks on a person. After somebody makes a purchase, reach out to that person to see where they stand in terms of customer satisfaction. Offer to feature the individual on your page displaying the product or the results of the product. You do not need to bribe anybody with the promise of monetary compensation; being featured on a business page will likely be enough of an incentive for your customers to participate.

Monitor Tagged Photos

Instagram contains a feature known as tagging. This means that you can be tagged by other users in photos that have you in them. As a business, you might get tagged in customer photos that display your product or service. What you can be tagged in is up to your own discretion. Even if the photo has nothing to do with your business, if a user decides to tag you in it, it will appear on your profile. This is an interesting concept that can come with many perks and also many downfalls.

Being tagged in a customer photo is normally going to be a great, organic marketing technique. This person likely posted an image and tagged you because they are satisfied with what they received. When other people seek out third party opinions, a way to do this is by browsing your tagged photos. The content is like a built-in advertisement for your brand. Alternatively, this can also work against you. If a customer has a bad experience and decides to tag you, this will also show up on your page.

Maintaining the highest level of customer service is important. If anyone is dissatisfied with something that they purchased from your company, you should do your best to reach out to that person to try and remedy the situation. Think about your tagged photos as another form of Yelp reviews; there can be good ones, bad ones, and everything in between.

Privacy Settings

The easiest way to monitor your tagged photos is by changing your privacy settings. Instagram offers you the chance to add these photos onto your profile manually. This means that when you get tagged in something, you will have to review it first. Having control over your tagged photos can save you the embarrassment of a potential bad post. However, the best approach is to do your best to make your customers happy before a negative post is created.

If you already have some unfavorable tagged photos or if you simply want to control what is on display, you can hide images from your profile. Instagram is all about customization, and this feature allows you to select how you would like to represent yourself. Get rid of the tagged photos that are negative or include spam. An example of a spam-like post would be something that you are tagged in that is not relevant to your business. Nobody likes wading through spam while browsing Instagram, so save your followers the hassle.

Etiquette

Just as you are particular about what tagged photos best represent your company, other users are too. Make sure that you follow a certain level of etiquette when it comes to tagging other people in photos. Tagging people in your photos is a way for you to gain popularity, but this won't always work in your favor if you abuse the privilege. A lot of people try to tag famous users in their posts in order to get noticed on that user's tagged photos page. This is bothersome for more than one reason.

A lot of the time, a famous user is going to have tagged photos monitored for approval. If this isn't the case, there is normally a lot of spam found. Don't simply tag a user because you want to ride the wave of their popularity. This will come across as annoying. Also, your post is likely going to get lost in all of the other photos that the user is tagged in for the same purpose. Only tag someone in your photo if that person is relevant to what you are posting.

However, there are some exceptions. If you are making a post about influential people who have inspired your brand, this is a great time to utilize the tagging system. Use your best judgement when it comes to this. Privacy is an important aspect of social media. Even though Instagram was created so that you can share your life, experiences, and business, there is still a certain level of privacy that needs to be maintained.

If a customer sends you a results photo but asks not to be tagged, respect their wishes. The photo might be unflattering to the individual or they might simply want to remain anonymous. The best thing to do is ask for their permission to tag them in the photo. The worst-case scenario is that you will receive a "no" response and then you can move on.

Don't Disappear Without Warning

Gaining followers on Instagram extends beyond the initial follow; you need to give your followers a reason to stay. Just as posting too much can drive people away, the same happens when you don't post enough. Make sure that you have a goal in mind for your Instagram account. Even if you aren't posting every single day, make sure that you plan to post at least a few times each week. Not only will this keep you relevant, but it will also keep you displayed by the algorithm.

Accounts that appear inactive or hardly used are pushed down by the algorithm. This means that the outreach of an account that posts weekly will be more successful than that of one that only posts every other week. Remember, Instagram does take work. If you can't be consistent with your posts, it wouldn't be a bad idea to look into hiring a social media marketing manager to help.

If you know that you are going to be absent for some time, let your followers know! Think about your followers the way that you would your friends. If you had to go out of town, you would probably say something to your friends. The same applies on Instagram. This can be as simple as addressing your absence in a caption. This becomes a placeholder, so your followers know that you will be returning with consistent content in the future.

Nobody likes following inactive accounts. You might notice that you lose followers when you post infrequently. This is why maintaining your posting schedule is an important factor when it comes to growing your following. If you take a look at the most successful accounts that you follow, it is likely that they post every single day. If you have something relevant to post each day, you can follow that strategy. Just make sure that you aren't spamming your followers.

Can You Purchase Followers?

If you have ever noticed a quick rise in popularity from a certain account, you might be left wondering how they did it. Working on posting relevant content each day, interacting with potential customers, and making sure that you are effectively advertising are all challenging aspects of becoming successful on the platform. Instagram does take work, despite what some might think. If you feel that your efforts are in vain, don't be so quick to jump to the conclusion that you are doing something wrong. There are ways that Instagram followers can be purchased, and this is a method that some businesses tend to gravitate toward because it is as easy as the click of a button.

There are several websites that promise you the exchange of followers for money. How can you know if the service is legitimate? Will the followers be interactive? In this instance, there are a lot of places that like to scam people by luring them in with the promise of popularity. Buying followers involves sharing information about your Instagram account. Naturally, this makes you vulnerable to hackers. You should be weary of who you share your account information with. Make sure that the company is reputable, or the person is someone that you trust. For example, if you hire someone to run your social media accounts, a social media manager is likely going to be a reputable source.

While many people do not believe in purchasing followers, it's an option that a lot of people choose to take. Sometimes, having the additional followers entices other accounts to follow you. It can be an effective marketing strategy if you are smart about it. The decision is entirely up to you as a business owner. Keep in mind that these followers for purchase are normally just shells of profiles; this means that the users are not real and will not interact with you. These empty accounts are created and maintained but do not actually have any ownership attached. When you buy followers this way, the only thing that will change is your follower count. You won't receive any additional interactions.

If you are okay with spending more money, some places offer followers for sale that are real accounts run by real individuals. With this type of purchase, you will have the chance of an interaction along with the rise in your follower count. Again, this is still not a guarantee since the accounts are all owned by real people who have their own interests and free will. Overall, buying followers is a form of temporary gratification and can be a big gamble. Instagram doesn't approve of the purchasing of followers, and regularly deletes these fake profiles, so you might not really be getting your money's worth.

In order to determine if buying followers is something you'd like to do, it's important that you first understand the pros and cons of doing so:

Pros

- **Your Numbers Will Rise**: The main benefit of purchasing followers is that your follower count will increase. This can help you out in several different ways from boosting you in the algorithm, to enticing people to check out your profile. People tend to pay more attention to accounts that appear popular.

- **It Speeds Up the Process**: Of course, there are plenty of ways that you can organically obtain followers, but they do take time. When you purchase followers, the result is instantaneous. For those who do not have as much time to spend on the platform, making a purchase like this can give you a great deal of social proof, quickly.

- **Marketing Will Be More Effective**: When you run ads based on your promoted posts, the potential customers that find your page will likely take note of your follower count. Seeing a business that has a large following can be one factor that encourages a person to make a purchase from you.

- **Credibility is Boosted**: Your reputation will grow as your follower count does. No matter how you obtain followers, brands and individuals alike will take you more seriously by default. A large follower count is normally a sign that you are doing something right.

Cons

- **The Accounts Aren't Run by People**: Most of the followers that you purchase are probably just going to be inactive accounts that were created and then abandoned. Because there are no users behind the account to run it, you won't get any of the interaction that is also needed for Instagram growth. If someone were to look at your followers and go to these accounts, they might catch on that they were purchased.

- **It Is a Fleeting Boost**: While your follower count will see immediate results, purchasing followers is nothing more than instant gratification. You will get the rise in numbers, but this does not mean that you won't have to work hard to maintain interest and make sales. Purchasing followers is merely an additional tactic when you are already working on a marketing campaign.

- **There Is a Stigma Involved**: A lot of people turn their noses up to those who decide to purchase followers. There is definitely a negative stigma involved, even though the decision is up to you to make. Anyone can buy followers, which does take away some of the credibility behind the accounts that choose to. If you decide that you still want to, mentioning it to others might not be the best idea.

- **Scams Are Very Common**: There are risks involved with purchasing followers. You will need to make sure that the company you are dealing with isn't just trying to scam you out of your money. It is very easy to promise a higher follower count without actually following through. If you find that you have compromised your information, change your password right away.

Chapter 4: How to Run Ads on Instagram

Advertising on Instagram is fairly simple once you get the hang of it. No matter what you would like to promote, it is likely that you will be able to do so with the help of Instagram's marketing tools. Because the ads do cost money to run, it is important that you follow the earlier steps that detailed how you should post effectively on Instagram. A post that is worthy of marketing should explain your mission clearly. The person should know what they are looking at when they see it and why they should buy it. If you do not want to promote sales, but simply want to spread the word about your business, the same clarity should apply. Let the customer know exactly what you do and why you do it.

Making the post is always the first step to advertising on Instagram; this is your base for the ad. Because it is going to be used in a professional way, make sure that the image is also up to par. You wouldn't want to select a mundane image to promote a great cause. Also consider what you put in the caption. Steer clear from anything vague or too informal. Your caption should include a call to action and more information about why the person reading it should take a look at your page and products.

Customizing Your Ad

When you have made a post that is worthy of being promoted, you get to decide how it will be shared. You have the objective of getting people to click on your post, and there are a few redirect targets that you can choose from. When someone clicks on your post, it can either take them to your page, to your website, or to your DMs. This part is up to you, as all of the above have their own benefits attached.

Linking to Your Page: If you want to give people the option to explore your page independently, it would be a good idea to let the ad redirect to your page. This way, people can browse through your posts and decide if your business is one that they want to follow or buy from.

Linking to Your Website: When your follower count isn't a main priority and you would rather focus on sales, consider linking directly to your website. This will take the user off of Instagram and onto your third-party website that features your products and services. Since the individual is already there, the chance of making a sale is increased.

Linking to Your DMs: This is a way to get people to interact with you one-on-one. Direct messages are used to communicate privately between Instagram accounts. If you are looking for feedback on your business or any aspect of it, running a targeted ad that focuses on this and then links to your DMs will be the answer.

Audience Specifications

The next step is to decide who will get to see the ad. Instagram gives you the option for an automatic draw, which means that they will select users for you. The ones that they pick will be similar to users that already follow you. They can determine this by common interests, what people like, who they interact with, and where they are located. Most people select this when they are just getting started, however, you can also create your own demographic.

To create your own target audience, you first get to decide where you want to run the ad. You can be as specific or as broad as you like. For example, if you are located in South Carolina, you can select cities such as Columbia, Charleston, Greenville, and Myrtle Beach. If you are more interested in having a widespread audience, you can select the entire state of South Carolina. There are benefits to both methods, and the one that you select will likely depend on the type of business that you run. If you provide a service that can only be obtained locally, it is better to stick with a specified radius.

If you do not want to list each city in your radius individually, Instagram allows you to put in an address and select a radius from there. You can enter your business address and select a 10-mile radius for the ad. It might take a little bit of experimenting to determine which method will work best for your business.

After you decide on a location, you are going to be given the option to select interests. This means that you can choose the keywords that your audience should have in common. For example, if you sell books, you could select the following interests: books, reading, and entertainment. Instagram encourages you to select a lot of interests so that a wide range of people will be reached by your ad.

The final specification involves selecting age and gender settings. This part is fairly straightforward. If you are selling makeup, you might want to target females aged 16-45, as an example. Depending on what kind of audience you are trying to attract, you should know who to target.

Budget

This part is arguably the most important; you need to decide how much money you would like to spend on the ad. This amount can be as little as $1, but keep in mind that the more money you put into the campaign, the better the outcome will typically be. You will also get the chance to select a duration. Instagram uses a sliding scale tool that makes it super easy to see what your estimated reach will be. You can set your budget and then change the duration to see which option will generate the most success for you.

The money is not deducted up front, but only when the ad stops running, so keep this in mind. You might put $50 into the campaign, but that money will remain in your account until it has been distributed over the amount of days that you have selected. Instagram's system works on a pay-per-click basis. This means that each time a user interacts with your post in a desired way (clicking on it and being redirected to your website, for example), a portion of the funds will be deducted from the budget. When all of the funds have been used, this is when Instagram charges you.

When you reach the confirmation page, you will get the chance to see a live example of how your promoted post will appear. This is also your chance to ensure that you understand exactly how much you will have to pay, the potential outreach results, and where your audience will be directed upon clicking. Instagram makes the process very easy, and you can pay for your ad using a credit card. If you are doing promotions regularly, you can keep a card on file and save your audience preferences for an easy way to create an ad quickly.

Monitoring

As your ad is running, you will be able to see its success along the way. Instagram gives you analytics on your ad that can be helpful when determining if your new clients are coming as a result of the ad. Under your "Ads Manager," you can click on your desired campaign name in order to see these statistics.

Because you can run more than one ad at a time, this is a handy way to stay organized. You will be able to view results relating to performance, demographic, and placement. If at any point you decide that you would like to extend the campaign, you can choose to add money to the budget and increase the duration.

What you should be looking for is the number of clicks that you are getting each day. The point of the ad is to encourage people to click on your post. You are essentially paying for Instagram to redirect traffic your way. On a business Instagram account, you are able to see how many weekly views you get on your profile. If your ad is redirecting to your profile, you should see this number increase while the ad is running. This is how you will know that it is working.

For posts that link to your website, use your own analytics tools to monitor your website traffic. Note how many sales you get for the duration of the ad campaign. Even if your ad does not result in a lot of additional sales, it can bring attention to your company in a widespread way. Running ads regularly will allow you to get noticed by people who might not have discovered your page organically. The targeted demographic and keywords ensure that your post is only being promoted to those who fit the certain criteria that you have created.

Advertising on Stories

As you now know, the stories feature on Instagram is a quick way for you to see what the people you follow are up to. People post photos and videos that disappear after 24 hours as a faster way to update Instagram without having to make a permanent post. The content that you post on your story is not limited to a certain format or theme. As a business, utilizing your story can benefit you in many different ways. You can post informal things, such as behind-the-scenes snippets. You can use your story to update your followers on general daily activity that goes on. People love to browse through stories because they are quick, and they change often.

While browsing through Instagram stories, they change from one user to the next automatically. Anyone who you follow that has posted a story will be added to this succession of temporary posts. This means that a single click can take you through hundreds of stories from every user that has posted one. In between every couple of stories, an ad is shown. This is how Instagram fits in sponsored posts and marketing campaigns. The ads are just as quick as the individual stories, only lasting for about 10 seconds.

As a business, you can choose to run your ad campaign in the form of an Instagram story instead of a post. Imaginably, this ad will be seen by a lot of different people who are browsing through stories. These ads can be shown to users that do not follow you. The process for creating this type of ad is the same as it is when you create a standard ad. You get to select your audience, keywords, budget, and duration. The same analytics tools are also provided for you to monitor the success of the ad.

Benefits

You might be left wondering which form of advertising is going to benefit your business the most. There are a couple of benefits that you get from choosing to advertise in a story rather than a post:

- **Quick Views**: It is much easier to view 100 stories rather than 100 posts on Instagram. Because they change automatically and only last a few seconds each, your ad will effortlessly be placed for other users to see. People normally do not have a very long attention span while they are browsing through social media, so the minimal amount of effort required is definitely a perk to advertising via Instagram stories.

- **Swiping Up**: When you select a redirect link on a story ad, the user simply has to swipe up on the screen if they would like to be redirected. There is no clicking necessary, which makes the task seem very easy. You can present all of the benefits of your product and then prompt the user to swipe up to learn more.

- **New Feature**: Being able to advertise on Instagram stories is a fairly new feature that was added in March of 2019. Because it is one of the newest ways to promote a business, a lot of companies have been finding success with it. This unique way to spread your message allows you to tell a story with the help of creative tools that can alter your image with text options and interactive graphics.

Keeping Ads Intriguing

No matter which route you decide to take, running an ad involves creating content that is interesting enough for a user to click on. In order to do this, you need to present something that will catch a person's eye. Avoid drab color schemes and stock photos for your ad. As you know, the same concept applies to creating Instagram posts; use images that are clear and high quality. A person should know exactly what is being shown when they look at the photo or video. You are allowed to take artistic liberty here, so don't be afraid to make edits on your content. When you find the right image, you can enhance it with the tools that Instagram provides. If you want to take a more professional route, you can even hire a graphic designer to spruce it up.

Text and Color

If you decide to put text over the content, keep it to the point. Nobody is going to want to read through a paragraph of words when trying to view an image. Focus on keywords and important details. If there is a discount or sale involved, be sure to mention this. Customers are drawn in by the idea that they are receiving something special because they are seeing the ad. Make sure that the font style and color that you choose are legible. Gravitating toward neon colors might not be the smartest advertising decision.

Your color scheme matters. Once you have a legible font, pick a color that won't clash too much with the image. If your brand already has a color scheme, try to stick to it for the sake of staying cohesive. The ad that you create should be something that you can post onto your page without it looking out of place. If you don't have a particular color scheme in mind, go for something that is easy on the eyes.

Concepts

It isn't a bad idea to produce a concept for your ad before you actually create it. How do you want your audience to feel? This is always a smart thing to consider before making a post of any kind. Sometimes, the ad is going to be to direct, with a clear objective of making sales. Other times, you might find that you want to elicit a different kind of response from your audience.

Maybe you want to express how your product is benefitting the industry. Another thing to focus on can be the way that your company gives back to society. There are plenty of ways to draw attention to your brand without flat out asking the audience to make a purchase.

Draft out several different ad concepts that you can use. It will be smart to have these on hand in case you need to create an ad on short notice. People enjoy hearing the story behind the brand. Consider sharing how your company came to be. Maybe there is a particular way that you would like to help people with your products. These angles can be used to make the ad seem less like a sales pitch.

Observation

If you are having trouble coming up with new designs and concepts, take a look at the ads that pop up on your feed. You can learn a lot from your competitors. Each time you notice an ad, take a look at the number of interactions that it has. Noteworthy ads will likely have elements in common; this is what you need to be observant about. If you know what kind of ads are successful on Instagram, you can turn the template into one that will fit your own brand. You don't want to directly copy other companies; this might cause some problems. Instead, take note of what works and see how you can put your own unique spin on it.

Instagram also gives you the ability to see what your followers are liking and commenting on. Use this to observe what people gravitate toward. You will be able to create your ad with this knowledge of what is currently in demand. While Instagram can seem like a fun way to pass the time, it can be a lot more than that if you are a business who is advertising on the platform. The ease of access to all of this information makes it an extremely innovative way to research what is popular and to apply it to your own business.

How Often Should You Advertise?

Because Instagram makes it so easy, you are probably wondering how often you should create ad campaigns. The answer revolves around a few different factors. First, you need to consider your budget. Sometimes, companies that are just starting out do not have the extra spending money to advertise. Even if you can only afford to run 1 ad each month, that is still a starting point. This small boost can grow your brand little by little. Of course, minimal advertising is going to provide minimal results. Try to set aside at least $20 each month from your sales that you can put towards your marketing campaign. It will pay off in the long run.

If money is not your main concern, it is a smart idea to create a schedule for your ads. You won't just want to promote every single post that you make. This will defeat the purpose of appearing intriguing to your audience. Remember, you don't want to come across as spam. Instead, pick 2-3 posts that you would like to promote each week. Make sure that they are your best posts. The ones that you promote are the ones that best represent your brand's online presence. Your aim is to interest users enough to the point that they decide to follow you. Getting clicks is great but earning a follow or a new customer is even better.

When you notice a specific campaign is doing well, continue to format your ads that way. The trick to Instagram is to utilize something until it is no longer popular. This is the way that most social media platforms operate, both in personal use and business use alike. As long as you are doing continuous research, it shouldn't be too difficult to remain current and relevant. Don't be afraid to think outside of the box, too. Being creative can often work in your favor on Instagram. Showing the audience something that they haven't seen yet can boost your following.

Comparative Advertising

When you have different options at hand, you might be wondering why you should advertise on a social media platform rather than going with a more traditional approach. Nowadays, more people are on social media than ever before. Instagram is not only limited to a Millennial audience. Instead, you will be able to find kids, their parents, and even their grandparents on Instagram. As mentioned, the audience already exists. One of the hardest parts about advertising is knowing where to share your business. Paying for an ad agency to run your campaign in a magazine or on some third-party website most likely isn't going to be as effective as what Instagram advertising can offer.

Instagram is a self-sufficient platform that does not concentrate on selling. Because it actually promotes sharing life experiences, users are able to browse in a more relaxed way. When the audience is casual, they are far more likely to take a true interest in your business. Many people are put off by direct sales pitches, and utilizing social media for your advertising needs can eliminate that issue if your ads are designed correctly.

Customization

Another way that Instagram ads triumph over traditional ads is by allowing you to customize the entire process. Social media allows you to customize your target audience in a diverse way. Utilizing the keywords that Instagram already tracks can save you time and money by avoiding running your ad to people who do not have an interest in your type of business. Instagram allows you to choose an extremely specific target audience to promote to, so that your advertising budget isn't wasted on people who have no interest in your products.

Analytics Tools

During every step of the way, you are able to view the statistics on your ad through Instagram's built-in tools. When you use traditional advertising, you don't get this much insight into the success of your campaign. You are left to guess where your customers came from and how they heard about you. Instagram makes this very clear by showing you how many people click on your ad and how many times it has been viewed. You are able to track patterns of activity in order to better customize campaigns in the future.

Price Point

By traditional advertising standards, Instagram comes in at a lower price point. If you think about the amount of money you pay for the exposure you can get, it is clear to see that this is a great deal. With the sliding scale options, you only have to pay exactly what you are able to within your given budget. Even for as little as $1, you can create an ad that will gain you new followers. This isn't an option in traditional advertising. Often, you must agree to pay a flat fee up front in order to run an ad. Instagram only charges you once your ad is clicked on, giving you the security of knowing that it is being seen.

Exposure

Even if you are simply making a post on Instagram, this is also a form of advertising. Posting on the platform is free for all users. If you decide that you would like to inform others about your business and what you have to offer, you can do so without spending a penny. While the outreach isn't nearly as broad, a lot of companies find success in simply making regular posts on Instagram. This is another way that traditional advertising just cannot compare. Social media gives us all the option to share what we want to, and in turn, this can lead to popularity and even sales.

Making Connections

Not only can you get to know your customers on social media, but you can also meet companies or people that you can collaborate with in the future. Instagram advertising goes beyond just selling products. There are plenty of users who seek out collaboration opportunities as a mutually reciprocated way to advertise. When someone else posts about your business on their profile, this gives you a boost in notoriety. This is a very easy way to grow your account, and not to mention, it's also free. Be open to talking with users on Instagram because you never know what kind of business opportunity can unfold.

Evolution

Judging by the rate that Instagram has grown in the last few years, it is not expected to slow down anytime soon. From gaining more users daily to creating new uses for their technology that have never been seen before, it is only going to keep getting better. Advertising on Instagram means that you are attempting to stay current on the marketing front. Creating an account on Instagram has always been free, and it is a powerful tool for growing your business. Regular app updates ensure that its creators are working constantly to provide users with the best social media experience. Instagram continues to be one of the most regularly and widely used apps worldwide.

Chapter 5: Influencer Marketing

Influencer marketing is likely a term you have heard a lot in the last few years. What does it mean to be an "Influencer?" By definition, an influencer is someone who makes an impact on a niche topic. A lot of Instagram influencers succeed in the beauty industry, advertising makeup and skincare on their pages. Anyone can be an influencer, but despite what some think, it does require a lot of work. Because you must be seen by a wide range of people, gaining popularity on Instagram is one of the steps that must be taken. Having a decent number of followers is essential to spreading your message. Sometimes, this social media notoriety comes from simply posting quality content. Plenty of people are put into an influencer role without even intending on it in the first place.

How can Instagram influencers assist you with growing your brand? There are actually several ways that you can collaborate with these users in order to make the most of their large followings. From sponsored posts to mutual collaborations, getting into influencer marketing is by far one of the smartest business decisions you can make while you are using Instagram as an advertising platform. The best part about this type of work is that, oftentimes, it is free or quite cheap. With the promise of a shout out, tag, discounted, or free product, many influencers will be willing to work with you.

Collaborations

A collaboration is exactly how it sounds; it is a way for you to join forces with another user in order to gain exposure. For a typical collaboration, this can look like two accounts making similar posts where they mention each other. It can involve something simple like tagging the user in your post or using a hashtag. The details of the collaboration are at your discretion. This step should be sorted out directly with the person or company that you intend on working with. Instagram never interferes in these instances and will simply provide you with the platform to create them. An example of this can appear as such:

If you have a clothing company and you would like to collaborate with a model, you can offer to send her a t-shirt in exchange for a post. The model can make a post wearing your brand and tag your account. You can also post this same photo on your account, creating double outreach.

This becomes especially beneficial when the other user has a large following. A lot of Instagram models work hard to maintain a certain follower count, so it is a good idea to start there if you want to create a collaborative effort. There are no rules when it comes to approaching someone for a collaboration. The worst possible outcome is that you will be declined. Don't let this discourage you! There are millions of users on Instagram, so keep reaching out until you find the right opportunity.

Outreach

Knowing what to say is an important first step when it comes to collaborations. You should have a clear idea in mind, and you should also keep in mind what type of trade you would like to accomplish. This might involve sending someone your product for free or at a discounted rate in exchange for a post. No matter how you want to set up the trade, make sure that you stand firm with your boundaries. Some people might test you to see if you are able to be taken advantage of. If you only want to trade one product for one dedicated post, then make sure your terms are clear.

Reach out to several influencers at once. This not only gives you more of a chance at getting a positive response, but it also keeps your options open. When people find out that they aren't the only candidate for the job, this might be further incentive for them to work with you. Create a little bit of a friendly competition. Direct messaging is the best way to communicate these terms with users on a private level. If you are open to receiving applications, you can make a post or a story about the search. This way, people who see it will decide to message you if they think they can fill the role.

Even though collaborating isn't exactly a business deal, it would be wise to draft up a simple contract that outlines what you expect of the other user. Make sure that these expectations are clear and also note what form of "payment" you will be providing. Some companies don't mind paying for this type of advertising out of budget. If you are just starting out, you might not have the means to do this. Trade work is widely accepted on the platform, so it is definitely not mandatory to compensate in that way. The timeline is also important to include. You don't want to be waiting for months to see a post after you have already sent over your product, so ensure that there is a deadline that works for everyone involved.

When you find the influencers that you would like to work with, make sure that their vision aligns with your company's in some way. It wouldn't make sense to seek out an influencer who focuses on fitness routines to collaborate with a donut shop. Much like the content that you post, your collaborations should also be on brand. Take the time to explain a brief amount of information about your company; keep this short and to the point. Remember, you don't want your message to come across as spam. Once this is explained, you can ask the user if there is an interest in a collaboration. Send a contract over once you receive a "yes" response.

Be Picky

If you publicly express your desire to collaborate with others, an influx of users might approach you. Some people only care to gain attention on Instagram. While this is okay on a personal level, you should be picky about who you decide to work with from a business standpoint. It is okay to say no; you do not have to work with every single person who expresses an interest in your brand. Being in this position allows you time to do a bit of research. When people reach out to you offering to advertise your product, take a look at their page.

A lot can be gathered from a brief glance at someone's account. Is their content filler or quality? Do they have a large following? What type of interests do they express? This is all very important when you are seeking out an influencer. Steer clear of anyone controversial. With the way that social media news can spread so quickly, your business might end up in the unintentional crossfire. You should be able to assess what type of person you are dealing with by the way they are presented on social media.

On Instagram, everyone gets to choose to put their best self forward. It really says a lot about a person if you notice that they are deciding to focus on negativity. For the sake of your professional reputation, stay away from users like this. Those who spread the message of kindness and inclusivity are going to provide the best type of collaboration for your brand.

Creative Control

During your collaboration, creativity can be utilized. Instead of approaching an influencer with a simple request to make a post, you can come up with a concept that can be meant to attract an audience in a more involved way. Maybe you'd like to get people to use a certain hashtag or take a photo in a certain location and tag your brand. There are several things that you can come up with to make the collaboration more fun and interactive. Think of this as a call to action in the form of an ad.

The possibilities are endless when it comes to creativity on social media. Approaching someone with an idea rather than an open-ended offer is a lot more promising. You can even suggest that the influencer provide you with feedback on the creative direction of the collaboration. Working together in this way will build trust and an honest connection. You might decide that you want to work together again in the future, so it is best to keep the lines of communication open.

There is nothing black or white about collaborating. Because Instagram has very minimal guidelines on what is unacceptable to post, you have the freedom to express yourself in ways that aren't always possible in traditional advertising. Using another person to help you is one of the best resources available. People like to see real examples of things, and seeing your product being used by an influencer is a great way to accomplish this.

Feedback

The way that you wrap up a project can be just as important as the way you start it. After the collaboration is over, make sure that you thank the influencer that you worked with. It feels nice to be appreciated and it is very easy to send a follow up message after everything is complete. If you would like to work with this person again, it is worth mentioning that. You might be able to begin the creative process of coming up with your next collaboration idea together.

Let the influencer know how well the collaboration went in terms of figures. While you don't have to disclose sales figures if you choose not to, it can be beneficial to share any updates of the view count and follower count that you noticed. This is another form of gratification to the person that you worked with; it shows that their efforts have made a difference to the growth of your company.

Ideally, the sharing of this information should be mutual. Ask the influencer if they would be willing to share the same figures with you. By seeing how well your collaboration went, you will know if it is worth it to do another one that is similar. The more information that you have, the better you will be able to understand the analytics from the project.

Benefits of Influencer Marketing

As a business on Instagram, you technically do not need to follow a set of rules in order to be successful. There are; however, plenty of benefits from working with an influencer as a part of your marketing plan. Utilizing the help of another person is always a great way to increase exposure. On Instagram, your main goal should be to get recognized by the largest relevant audience possible, and influencers are one of the best ways to achieve that.

Constant Exposure

If you were to scroll through your news feed right now, you will likely come across a post made by an influencer. The great thing about influencers is that they blend in with the patterns that are already visible on Instagram. From what is trending to what is aesthetically pleasing, an influencer normally has a firm grasp on what is currently going to attract attention. You might not even realize that a post you are viewing is a collaboration. This is a good thing, because when you decide to market your product this way, other users won't see it as a traditional form of advertising. As it has been explained, people like to see products being used in real time with real opinions.

Instagram has a very high engagement rate when compared to other social media platforms. This is largely due to the ease of interacting with other users. With a few simple clicks, you are able to like, share, and follow. Instagram focuses less on what is said (as compared to Facebook and Twitter) and more on what is seen. It is a visual portal to just about any niche.

Trust

If your friend were to recommend a movie to you, would you be likely to check it out? This same concept is how influencer marketing is intended to work. While influencers are not really "friends" with all of their followers, they make it a point to become as relatable as possible in order to earn trust. When someone with a large following makes any kind of recommendation, a good handful of people are probably going to listen. Even if there is skepticism, this still creates a conversation about the product at hand.

This type of connection is a huge advantage that is unique to social media. Before this, there was never a comparable form of advertisement. Users can interact with the influencer and ask questions about why the product is being recommended. Not only do you have the opportunity to garner more sales, but you also have the ability to educate the audience on your brand via a popular third party.

Authenticity is important when it comes to trust; this is why you must be selective with the influencers that you decide to work with. The collaboration needs to make sense, or else it loses some of its value. You wouldn't want to hire a hunter to vouch for your vegan food line. Pay attention to your niche and try to find influencers who share the same or similar views. With the growing number of users on Instagram, this shouldn't be too much of a challenge.

Small Scale

Don't feel that you need to hire an influencer with millions of followers who is going to charge you money to collaborate. The great news is that there are plenty of different levels of influencers. "Micro-influencers" are a group of people who have a decent following (typically several thousand) and likely will be happy to trade a discount or some free product for making a post. Because this type of influencer is also concerned about growing, it will be more like a mutual collaboration that thrives on exposure. As a smaller business, it makes sense to seek out smaller influencers at first. You can work your way up to bigger collaborations as your following grows.

Being a micro-influencer does not come with a celebrity status attached. Instead, this type of influencer will often appear more trustworthy and relatable. It can be a smart business strategy to work with these smaller scale individuals. The best type of influencers to work with will have an interesting feed that doesn't seem too curated or faked. A lot of bigger influencers will often appear as though they are living a seemingly perfect life that is taken directly from a magazine. Most people find this less relatable. Even though an influencer with millions of followers will have a larger outreach, the percentage of their followers that actually click on their posts can be lower than with most micro-influencers. While this isn't true for all large influencers, it is something to be aware of.

Things to Keep in Mind

With any business decision, always aim to protect your reputation and your brand. The promise of exposure and "free" advertisement can be tempting on Instagram. Some of it really is too good to be true, though. There are several things that you need to be aware of as a business-owner on Instagram:

- **Fake Followers**: Just as you have learned earlier, anyone can purchase followers. Aside from the empty profiles that are used to generate larger follower counts, there are also followers that are actually bots. These accounts are run by an algorithm that is designed to interact with users in a pre-programmed way. When you are deciding on an influencer to collaborate with, it is a smart idea to take a look at some of their followers' profiles. If you notice a lot of bots or fake profiles, it might not be the best idea to collaborate with this user. If you do, your brand is just going to end up being advertised to an audience that cannot interact or make a purchase.

- **Engagement Rates**: This goes hand-in-hand with the quality of someone's followers. Take a look at how much engagement the influencer gets. If you notice that there are 200 likes on a picture that belongs to a user with 12,000 followers, then something isn't adding up. It could be because the followers are fake, purchased, or bots. This is another indication of how your collaboration will succeed (or fail).

- **Payment Arrangements**: With any type of collaboration, you must emphasize clearly what your form of "payment" is going to be. If you decide that you are going to work with someone, make sure that it is made clear what they can expect in return. This is why contracts can come in handy; they can outline the job in writing so that there is no confusion in the future. This also prevents someone from claiming you were going to pay them with monetary compensation when what you initially agreed upon was a trade.

- **Beware of Scams**: While Instagram is a fun place, it can also be full of untrustworthy people looking to scam you of your time, money, and efforts. When you are sharing business information, make sure that you are sure of the other person's intentions. Never allow anyone access to your account; this is one of the easiest ways to lose it. Arrange a formal payment method if a payment is going to be sent. You will want to make sure that there is a receipt for the transaction.

Rules and Regulations

While there are limited restrictions on what you can and cannot post on Instagram, there are some standards that must be met regarding influencer marketing types of posts. The Federal Trade Commission regularly monitors sponsored posts on social media. It is important that you are following these requirements so that you can inform influencers of what the post needs to consist of. This is possible with a small amount of research done on your end. It is best to become educated on the topic before you begin working with other users.

FTC Compliance

The FTC is a government organization that is responsible for the protection of the consumer. As a business owner, it is important that your business practices do not intentionally deceive customers. The FTC scans social media for these deviations. It also ensures fairness in the marketplace. For example, a company should not have a majority of the control in any given industry. This makes for an unfair monopoly. The FTC believes that the consumer has a right to know if a post is sponsored, and they have taken many steps in recent years to make sure that this is properly disclosed.

If a post is not labeled as sponsored or as a collaboration, consumers might form the wrong impression about the brand being discussed. While a lot of influencers do genuinely use or enjoy the products that they are promoting, that is not always the case. A post without a disclosure might mislead a consumer, and this is exactly why the FTC monitors social media posts. You might be wondering how you can keep your business in compliance with these terms.

The most important thing to remember is transparency. If an influencer is working with you to promote your product or vice versa, talk about it. Mentioning the collaboration is a form of being transparent with the audience. They will realize that both parties formed an agreement to promote one another. It is up to you as a business owner to ensure that the influencer is aware of any FTC rules that must be followed. This all depends on the type of post that is being made.

Using hashtags such as #ad or #sponsored is a popular way to disclose a collaboration. This is a very normalized form of using hashtags nowadays and both are FTC compliant. The FTC believes that the hashtags clearly represent the intentions of the posts, leaving no guesswork to be done by the consumer. They prefer if the hashtag is placed near the beginning of the caption, not hidden among your other extensively used tags. This isn't the only way to properly disclose the information, though.

If you feel that using the above tags are too formal, you can create your own. A lot of companies like to use a template of #brandnamepartner. For example, Starbucks uses

#Starbuckspartner on their posts. This will make you stand apart from the other ads on Instagram while still staying true to your brand. Even if you are not sure if your posts warrant this type of disclosure, it is better to be safe than sorry. Encourage all influencers that you collaborate with to clearly mention the terms of the post.

For those who wish to forgo hashtags altogether, there is another way that the partnership can be disclosed. A caption by the influencer that thanks you for gifting them the product is an indication that you are working together. A simple thank you is not good enough for the FTC, however. You must also make sure that the statement alludes to the fact that the item was given as a gift or as a trade of some sort.

Even if nothing is actually paid to the influencer for collaborating with you, this fact must be disclosed in some way. Mentioning that the item was complimentary in the caption is a way to do this.

Disclosures in Stories

Providing proper disclosures in Instagram stories can look slightly different than the disclosures that are made on regular posts. One of the main reasons is that Instagram stories do not have a designated spot for captions. It is up to the user to add text to properly explain the photo or video that they have posted. There are creative ways that influencers can get this done without sounding too commercialized. From creating colorful text to using keywords, this can be done in a way that still appears genuine to the audience.

A popular way of doing this is by showing an "unboxing" of the item(s). This does several things all at once. The audience is shown that the user has received these products directly from a brand, a genuine reaction by the influencer is provided, and it is an entertaining category of content that is currently very popular among Instagram users. The same rules apply in terms of using hashtags or deliberately adding text to stories to indicate the partnership. A combination of these two will ensure that you are in compliance when a story is posted.

Work Your Way Up

Much like growing your Instagram account, you will need to work your way up to large collaborations. It is very rare to get the opportunity to work with large-scale influencers from the beginning of your marketing efforts due to the demand that is already in place. Influencers that have a large following are normally approached on a daily basis with collaboration offers. It can be hard to own a smaller business while trying to compete with these other brands that want to work with the influencers.

Reaching out to people who are micro-influencers can be a great starting point, along with advertising on your page that you are willing to collaborate with others. Working on these smaller collaborations will earn you the credibility and the following that you will need if you want to work on larger collaborations in the future.

Don't get discouraged if you cannot find influencers to collaborate with at first. Keeping in mind the quality of the content that you need, the authenticity of the audience, and the values of the influencer, you'll need to make sure that the given business relationship is going to be the right fit. It is a lot to consider all at once. Not settling until you find the perfect person to collaborate with is going to be a very helpful approach when attempting to grow your following.

Chapter 6: Examples of Businesses That Have Used Instagram Marketing Effectively

Learning by example is always one of the best ways to learn. This is especially true with social media. If one method of advertising works well for a business, it can be wise to take notes on what they are doing.

In this chapter we'll take a look at some companies that have used Instagram marketing successfully. These are just a few notable examples, and if you have a look at your own Instagram feed, you'll surely come across countless other companies that are using social media marketing to their advantage!

Sprint

The first thing that Sprint did right was choosing popular influencers to help spread the word about their campaign. The Live Unlimited Campaign focused on influencers who already fit the narrative of the message they were trying to portray. Their new inclusive plan advertised that no matter if you were into stunts, sports, comedy or beauty, you were going to want to document these the things that were of interest to you. With the help of well-known YouTube and Instagram influencers, Sprint was able to get this message across. In a culture that revolves around documenting and sharing moments with friends, family, and even the world, their campaign was widely successful in attracting a young audience.

Success Factors

- **A Natural Fit**: Sprint's campaign was successful because of the influencers that they selected. The group did not have the largest following nor were they the most talked about, but they fit the message that was already in place. Sprint wanted to show some diversity, and by way of these influencers, they were able to do so while getting their advertising message across.

- **Young Generation**: The aim of the campaign was largely focused on a group of people, who were called Generation Z. By creating a marketing campaign with a select demographic, Sprint knew that the content would have to appeal to the crowd. The audience was meant to be a vibrant and inquisitive group that had a lot of influence over what is going on in the world.

- **Personal Narratives**: With the Live Unlimited Campaign, Sprint did not try to script the influencers or direct the content too much. They wanted it to be genuine and it focused on the real-life stories of the people involved. This is a way to create a personable approach while advertising. The audience never felt like they were being sold a product, but instead, were learning about their favorite popular voices.

Old Navy

The popular clothing chain created their own type of influencer marketing when they launched their 2018 Black Friday campaign. Old Navy is no stranger to the industry, being a prominent source for children's and adult's casual wear. They decided to focus the campaign on regular people that they considered to be influential. Selecting a celebrity endorsement from a retired Yankees player, Old Navy incorporated a charitable act into their advertisement strategy. The aim was to raise money for the Boys & Girls Club of America.

Alex Rodriguez, the retired MLB star, was a former member of the non-profit. He ended up helping the company raise $1,000,000 that went to the worthy cause. This portion of sales that ended up going to charity was grossed on the one day alone, which was an amazing effort. Doing a good deed will get you far if you can incorporate it into your marketing strategy.

Success Factors

- **One Influencer**: Old Navy, despite being a large company, decided to keep their strategy minimal. They went with only using one influencer to help spread the word about their campaign. Also, they selected a very short window of time to complete this. Because Black Friday is a huge day in the retail industry, they knew that they had to approach with something hard-hitting.

- **Charitable Act**: A lot of the time, more people will listen to you as a brand when they know that your marketing involves helping out a good cause. This was an excellent approach made by Old Navy. The promise of helping children in need by purchasing merchandise on Black Friday was enough to fuel sales and assist a great cause.

- **Staying Simple**: One of the most common mistakes with influencer marketing is trying to convey too much to the audience. Sometimes, the content will be so highly saturated that it can become confusing what the actual message being portrayed is. Old Navy clearly expressed that the result of making a purchase would mean a contribution to the cause. This is often enough incentive to drive sales without needing to use gimmicks or exaggeration.

Naked Juice

A niche brand that has recently grown in popularity over the last decade, Naked Juice, decided to try out a campaign where they would use the sponsored post feature on Instagram to advertise. On these posts, they utilized the help of a popular lifestyle blogger to share their vision with the world. Their tactic was to have Kate La Vie create content that she normally would while incorporating a bottle of the juice somewhere in the photo. This minimally clever tactic turned out to work well in their favor.

While Naked Juice had the option to be front and center in their advertising, they opted for a more subtle approach. They did not want the juice to be the main focus of the ad. Instead, they tried a more subliminal approach by making it just one of the components. This drove an audience to the brand that might not ordinarily have gravitated toward it.

Success Factors

- **Subliminal Approach**: Without being deceptive, Naked Juice drew the audience in to their product without directly focusing on it. This is a great technique to use in advertising because it allows the audience to feel that they are coming to a conclusion on their own.

- **Diverse Lifestyles**: Seeing the juice being advertised

among other lifestyle elements shows the audience that having the product makes sense. Not everyone can relate to the influencer's lifestyle, but it shows that she was able to incorporate the product, making it seem possible for others. This type of content can inspire someone, causing a change in their lifestyle.

- **Easy to View**: The simplicity of the sponsored posts made the content quite easy on the eyes. The use of a particular aesthetic can be successful since Instagram is a visual platform. Naked Juice kept this in mind when they decided which influencer they were willing to work with. Kate's account is filled with posts that feature the same aesthetically pleasing features and style.

Loeffler Randall

Even high-end brands utilize the benefits of influencer marketing, proving that the concept is suitable for all brands. Loeffler Randall sells high-end shoes and accessories that have risen in popularity largely thanks to the decision that they made to advertise on Instagram. Word spread fast about their products, and they became a must-have on the list of several well-known influencers.

LR created their own ambassador campaign. They did their best to select individuals who were diverse and creative. One of their main groups of influencers turned out to be creative businesswomen. A powerful message was spread throughout this campaign, inspiring others along the way. The ambassadors could be seen posing in photos wearing LR merchandise while using the custom hashtag that the company assigned. This cohesive mix of organization and inspiration led to a great amount of success for the brand.

Success Factors

- **Niche Influencers**: LR did something right by narrowing down the criteria for what they were seeking in an ambassador. By choosing a powerful group of creative women, their message was able to speak for itself. They wanted to find go-getters; people who were strong and could independently represent the brand.

- **Unique Hashtag**: The hashtag that was used during the campaign makes it unmistakably recognizable. As discussed, hashtags play a central role when it comes to marketing on Instagram. Users knew what the posts were representing right away by viewing the hashtag.

- **Expanding the Audience**: Even though the brand itself is in the high-end category, they decided to select influencers of many different backgrounds and career paths to represent the products. This diversity often goes over well on Instagram, especially when it can be utilized in a marketing campaign.

Glossier

Glossier is a beauty brand that is known for their no-nonsense products. It is a female-owned company that aims to bring back simplicity to the makeup industry, while providing products that deliver. The brand was started as a digital effort, so it only makes sense that they would utilize social media marketing to gain traction. Now also sold in physical locations, Glossier has seen a tremendous amount of growth in only a few years' time.

Their Regular Women Campaign was exactly what the name suggests; the company used the angle that all women are influencers. They did not want to utilize the help of big voices to spread the word about the company, but instead, they asked regular women to be the face of the brand. Given the incentive of a referral program that gives influencers a discount code, this is one way that Glossier got those with a large following to participate. It is a genius idea that highlighted diversity and inclusivity.

Success Factors

- **Inclusive Advertising:** There is nothing more inclusive than realizing that the brand relies on everyday women to spread the word about the products that they love. Glossier aims to have real people with genuine opinions as their influencers of choice. This alternative method of influencer marketing has garnered a lot of attention.

- **Reflecting Values**: Glossier is a self-made brand that was started by a young woman named Emily Weiss. Emily hoped that her marketing would be a reflection of the values and initiative that she possesses. By staying true to her own values as a business owner, this really shines through in the way that she operates her business.

- **Small Incentive**: Having something to offer those who can really make a difference in your business is a great idea. Something as simple as a discount code can entice people to want to work with the brand, but to also make purchases. Glossier really hit the nail on the head with this idea for their campaign.

Fiji Water

Even bottled water brands are on board with influencer marketing. Fiji started a campaign that featured Danielle Bernstein, a fashion blogger. Bernstein creates lifestyle content that focuses on clothing and feeling great about what you are wearing. The pair seem like an unlikely match at first, but the way that Fiji decided to approach the collaboration turned out to be great.

This campaign featured Bernstein completing exercise routines while fueling up with Fiji water. The way that this is all curated incorporated popular elements of today's culture, the brand's product, and a trendy influencer to explain the cause. All of these things contributed to the success of the campaign. By seeing Bernstein cool down with some Fiji water, the audience was encouraged to drink Fiji water during their own workout sessions.

Success Factors

- **Multiple Angles**: Fiji really nailed their campaign because they approached from multiple different angles. Not only did they show the product being used in a real-life situation, but they also motivated their audience to do the same. With Bernstein being the voice of reason, consumers could see why Fiji made sense as the choice of hydration.

- **Beneficial Content**: The workout videos that Bernstein completed were led by a professional personal trainer. Not only does the audience get a great product recommendation, but they leave the advertisement with some additional knowledge and the encouragement to get physically active in their own lives. This type of content does really well on Instagram.

- **Product Association**: When advertising a product, you want to make sure that you are sending the right message to your audience. Fiji wanted to convey that their water was perfect for feeling great and looking great. These are two very sought-after feelings that are craved by most individuals. By associating these positive feelings with their product, Fiji was able to see a lot of success in their marketing campaign.

Youfoodz

This brand is a different type of business that turned to influencer marketing; Youfoodz is an Australian fresh meal service. A trendy way to make sure that you are eating balanced meals, this type of company is a hit with Millennials. The company turned to the help of a whopping 80+ influencers to assist with the campaign. Consisting of Instagram posts and stories, Youfoodz hired these people to help with promoting their new Winter menu. With all of these different influencers helping promote the product, the audience was able to see plenty of different users eating the food.

Because the company revolves around a necessity, they felt it was important to show influencers of varying lifestyles using the product and highlighting how easy it is to incorporate Youfoodz into their daily lives. They maintained a focus on influencers who are in the health, fitness, and food niches.

Proving to be a worthwhile campaign, it gained attention from around 1.5 million users on the social media platform.

Success Factors

- **Aiming Broad**: Youfoodz decided that using only a handful of influencers wasn't enough, and instead, they partnered with more than 80 influencers. This was a decision that they made with the intention of spreading their message quickly and in a big way. Instead of running multiple campaigns over an extended period of time, they wanted to inform the audience about their limited product availability.

- **Extensive Hashtags**: A part of the campaign involved using plenty of hashtags. While this can be a hit or miss depending on the audience, Youfoodz had each of their influencers use these tags on their posts in order to promote the product. This is another example of how they did everything in their ability to make this one single campaign a success.

- **Niche Focused**: Food is not normally what we see advertised on Instagram. The usual makeup, fashion, and lifestyle posts tend to dominate the influencer marketing scene. Youfoodz took a risk that ended up paying off by deciding to turn to social media to reach a wide array of potential new customers.

Pedigree

Pedigree has remained a top pet food brand for a long time; it is a brand that many are already familiar with. They decided to create a campaign that would involve giving back, a great strategy that has proven to work by drawing on the kindness in people. It was called "Buy a Bag, Give a Bowl." Its aim was to encourage people to buy a bag of Pedigree, and then the company would provide a bowl of food to a dog in need. Understandably, people were very responsive to this campaign, considering that the impact of a purchase could help animals in need.

The influencers that were hired to make posts shared stories about their own pets, explaining what their animals meant to them. By doing so, Pedigree was seen as a more personable brand with good intentions behind their products. Consumers like to see authenticity, and Pedigree did an excellent job of being transparent enough to put theirs on display.

Success Factors

- **Good Cause**: Helping those in need is always going to make for a great cause that others will want to support. Pedigree chose a cause that made perfect sense given the industry that they are in. Their campaign was simple enough to gain traction and was enticing enough to encourage people to participate.

- **Breaking Barriers**: Having the influencers do something other than post the product in a controlled setting, and instead post a photo of a pet, was very effective. The campaign never felt like an advertisement, but instead a personal narrative. Its message was made clear in the form of a caption and dedicated hashtag, but the visual content was focused on something other than the actual product.

- **Dedicated Tagging**: Because the focus of this campaign was more personal, Pedigree chose to disclose it in the form of a hashtag. As we have gone over, this is a relevant way to inform the audience about the intention of the post while remaining FTC compliant. With assistance from the caption as well, this method seemed to work out well for Pedigree.

Pala Casino Resort & Spa

Even the hospitality industry can benefit from influencer marketing campaigns. Pala Casino Resort & Spa proved this. With one goal in mind, the resort decided to use the help of influencers to spread the word about their destination. They wanted to attract a younger crowd, so naturally, Instagram was the perfect place for this campaign to take place. Instead of simply sending influencers photos to post, they decided to do something larger – they held an event for 21 influencers to attend. From this event, the deal was that each one of them had to post 3 different photos to document the occasion.

This was a creative risk that took plenty of planning, but it paid off. Giving each influencer the chance to have some creative liberty during the campaign made for a lot of unique content. The incentive itself was great as well since the influencers were treated to a private party. Pala contacted Hollywood Branded for some help to facilitate the event.

Success Factors

- **Real Lifestyle**: Pala did not want to resort to the same photos of their resort that have already been posted countless times. They wanted new content, so they used the private event as a massive way to create it. Getting the influencers directly involved on site was a smart move by the company. It provided them a chance to truly experience the resort; therefore, resulting in authentic views about it.

- **Freedom of Choice**: The party was simply that, and the only requirements involved were the 3 posts per influencer. Each of these influencers were able to come to the resort and enjoy the event without feeling the pressure of the business deal. Its relaxed atmosphere was a great tactic to utilize and to obtain this real content.

- **Passive Advertising**: This form of marketing comes across in a way that purely suggests the benefits of staying at the resort. There were no gimmicks or promises of discounts. Pala wanted customers to see a realistic example of what resort life had to offer. An audience is normally very responsive to this type of advertising, feeling that they can imagine themselves living the same lifestyle.

What You Can Gather

Reading about the different ways that the above businesses have found success through influencer marketing should inspire you to get creative with your marketing efforts. There aren't any set rules when it comes to the creative guidelines of a marketing campaign. As long as you are being clear with your audience and are FTC compliant, you can come up with an endless number of ways to attract more customers and give your brand a fun appearance. No matter what type of campaign you produce, knowing about the trends in your given industry will always be important. Even if you do not directly follow or mention them, being aware of what is currently being discussed can provide you with insight on how you'd like to construct your own campaign.

Remember, Instagram is a social media platform that has the ability to change rapidly. With its growing number of users each day, there is the promise of several different things becoming "viral" on a regular basis. An influencer marketing campaign is supposed to show the audience your best features while putting a familiar face in the foreground. Whether the influencer has ten thousand or ten million followers, their content must be of consistently good quality. Think carefully about the influencers that you choose to represent your brand. You wouldn't want someone with questionable morals to direct the vision of your company, and this same theory applies with advertising.

How to Determine Success

Just because a photo gets an ample number of likes does not necessarily make it a "successful" campaign post. With the rate that users can buy followers, these interactions might not be the most genuine. While getting likes boosts your post in the algorithm, you cannot simply rely on them to earn new business. It takes a combination of the post gaining popularity as well as convincing the audience that you are a brand worthy of purchasing from before you will start to see success unfold. While there is nothing wrong with gaining followers during these campaigns, you will likely only want them if they are authentic accounts run by real people who are able to interact with you. These are the people that can become future customers.

Being adamant on tracking your analytics during the campaign is a key method to determine its success. As you already know, Instagram provides you with the ability to check on these figures. An increase in traffic is a wonderful thing, and this is especially true if you can tell that the users are discovering you due to posts made by an influencer. Be transparent with those you work with in sharing the results of each campaign. This is a motivational factor and it will also encourage the influencer to share the figures from his or her side, too.

Strategies

Reading about all of the above examples, you will find that there are so many strategies that you can use when it comes to creating your own marketing campaign. From who you choose to work with and what you advertise, this can make a big difference in the amount of interactions that you get. The following are some of the proven strategies that have worked for these businesses:

- **Incorporating Donations**: Whether you would like to give back to the community or help someone in need, allowing the customer to donate to a good cause while simultaneously purchasing your product is a great approach. Not only will this boost your sales, but it will also say something about the integrity of your company. In the future, people are going to remember this and what exactly it is that you stand for.

- **Using Multiple Influencers**: It is up to you as a company to decide how many influencers you would like to work with. Given the examples above, some choose to work directly with only one person while others have chosen nearly 100. There is no right or wrong answer when it comes to the amount of people that you choose to collaborate with. Having a plan for your campaign will shed some light on how many influencers you will need to utilize.

- **Getting Personal**: As a company, it can be hard to connect with all of your customers and potential customers on a more personal level. With the help of influencer marketing, you can allow some personal narrative to shine through while promoting your products. Many companies do this as a way to become closer to their audience. People appreciate this because it shows that you are more than just a brand; there is a real person or a team behind it.

- **Focused Demographic**: Much like boosting a post on Instagram, creating a campaign will also involve selecting a target audience. Sometimes, this can remain broad. When given a specific goal of reaching out to a certain group of people, the influencers that you choose can have a significant impact on this. For example, if you want to reach out to a tech-savvy crowd, consider going with someone who already maintains a successful tech account.

- **Aiming for Genuine**: Sometimes, it is necessary to provide the influencer with a lot of information about what exactly needs to be expressed in the campaign. An alternative approach is to hire influencers who already fit the narrative of the company. This means that their own personal story or lifestyle is used while also incorporating your product. Not only is this very effective, but it is also a lot less work than trying to make someone fit a mold.

- **Playing on Niches**: Thanks to its broad outreach, Instagram already contains thousands of niches. These are like categories that divide interests. Instead of having to create your own niche, you can find one that makes sense for your brand. By marketing to these people, you will be sure to receive a positive response in return. Many brands do research ahead of time to determine what niche would work best for them. For example, a bathing suit company could fall into several, such as: clothing, lifestyle, and beach. By deciding which one is trending the most, the campaign will ultimately become more successful.

- **Subliminal Advertising**: This is arguably one of the smartest marketing techniques, which allows the customer to feel that they are making the choice to buy your product without your influence. While this is not being deceptive in any way, using subliminal techniques, such as hiring an influencer to promote your product by displaying it in the background of their desirable lifestyle can give your audience the encouragement to make a purchase on their own. This is the exact opposite of the hard-selling technique that some older forms of advertising rely on.

- **Incentive-Based Sales:** It isn't wrong to offer your clients a form of reward for choosing to purchase from your brand. Some companies offer a discounted price for users who make purchases as a direct result of your marketing campaign. This is a really easy way to tell where your traffic is coming from, as well. If you assign your influencers a discount code to provide to the audience, you will be able to determine how many sales have come as a direct result of the campaign. Customers will also feel more valued knowing that they are a part of a special set of people that get to use the discount.

Chapter 7: Other Social Media Platforms to Use for Business Growth

While Instagram is a main contender, it is not the only social media platform that businesses have decided to utilize for their advertising needs. Plenty of businesses operate multiple different social media accounts for the purpose of spreading the word about their brand. One isn't better than the other; it simply depends on what type of goal you are trying to achieve. Taking a look at some of Instagram's direct competitors can give you an idea of where you can turn your focus. Whether you want to utilize one platform or seven, knowing about them all will ensure that you are up to speed on the benefits and features of each one.

Facebook

A platform that hardly requires an introduction, Facebook has remained a social media pioneer. In recent years, Facebook actually purchased Instagram. They are the larger entity behind the platform that you have been learning about. Facebook is a more interactive type of social media experience. Users are encouraged to not only share photos and videos with their friends and loved ones, but they also have the option to share status updates. These blurbs of thoughts can be anything from what is on a person's mind to an important cause that they think should be talked about.

Advertising on Facebook works in a similar way to advertising on Instagram, and this makes sense because the two platforms are affiliated. As a business, you will need to create a business account. This gives you the same access to analytics tools and advertising options that Instagram does. You can choose to "boost" or promote posts to an audience that you select the parameters for. The main difference between doing this on Facebook is that you can be a lot more interactive with your followers.

With an author Facebook page, you also get to share status updates, just like a personal page. You can update your followers on important information, share news about your products, and encourage interaction. Photos and videos can also be shared on the platform. There are several other ways to interact with your followers, like creating polls and attaching direct links. Facebook has expanded a lot in the last decade, encouraging users of all ages to join the platform. It isn't uncommon for entire families to each have their own accounts, ranging from children to grandparents.

Influencer marketing can be done on Facebook, too. The same rules of disclosure apply on collaborations and sponsored posts. If you are used to Instagram for your business marketing needs, learning how to utilize Facebook should be simple. The two are purposefully similar. Since the acquisition of Instagram in 2012, Facebook has seamlessly updated Instagram to create an easy to use interface.

Most businesses have a Facebook page by default. It is a common way to not only advertise but provide clients with a point of contact that isn't as formal as an email address or a phone number. The messaging feature allows clients to express comments or concerns in a way that is easier than ever. If you are unsure about which platforms that you would like to try for your business, Facebook should definitely be at the top of the list.

The great thing about social media is that, for the most part, it is free. Unlike advertising with an agency or through a different third party, you don't have to make a large investment. You can take it as seriously or as casually as you wish. Having a Facebook page for your business is a simple part of today's culture. Most people expect you to have one, and if you don't, your customers may even ask if you can make one. With how easy and beneficial a business page can be, there should be nothing preventing you from creating a page.

Anything that is challenging about Facebook can be overcome. You might feel at first that there are an overwhelming number of tools to choose from. If you think about this, it is a lot better than not having enough resources. Watch and learn from those around you; take a close look at what other businesses do.

Those who are successful are a great example of how you should approach your Facebook marketing campaigns. Just like Instagram, you also have the ability to think outside of the box. If you have an idea that you'd like to pursue, Facebook is a great place to try it out.

Twitter

A word-savvy social media platform, Twitter has been around for a long time. Founded in 2006, it has gone through different periods of popularity. Currently, Twitter stands among the top social media platforms. It can be put in a top 3 category alongside Instagram and Facebook. The main idea behind it is that it takes Facebook's status feature as its number one component. On Twitter, you get to share 280 characters of text on any topic that you find relevant. The platform is a way for users to sound off. While photos, videos, and GIFs can also be posted, a lot of people appreciate that Twitter mostly focuses on the text posts.

From these tweets, other users can like, comment, and re-tweet. The average timeline is filled with a wide variety of all of the above. You might be wondering, what can a business do on Twitter? There are actually several benefits to starting an account for your business. Most accounts on Twitter are going to look exactly the same even if it is for something that is work-related. You get to choose a handle and profile photo, create a short bio, and link to your website if you choose. The simplicity makes it an appealing choice for many business owners.

The only time you will notice a difference in accounts is when one contains a blue checkmark next to its username. This "verified" symbol is given to those with notoriety. It is not reserved for only A-list celebrities; many influencers and larger companies are able to obtain the small checkmark. The purpose of knowing if a profile is verified is to ensure that you are interacting with the real deal. Those with large followings can be at risk of copy-cat accounts. Because Twitter gives you the freedom to change your username and display name at will, people tend to try and fool other users.

When it comes to advertising, you have the ability to promote posts of your choosing. From the post that you create, you can click on a button indicating that you'd like to boost the post. You will be prompted to enter your payment info. The system works on a pay-per-click basis, much like the other large social media platforms. You will get to choose your audience and your keywords. Twitter's algorithm will strategically place your promoted post on timelines. All you have to do is decide what you want to say and who you want to say it to; Twitter takes care of the rest.

Another way to advertise on Twitter comes in the form of promoting your account. This works in a similar way to promoting a post, but instead, it is your account that is shown to other users by way of an algorithm. This is a great route to take if you are interested in growing your following. For this type of ad, you also get to select relevant keywords and choose target locations. This is a very passive form of advertising with the potential to produce great results.

The third way that you can advertise on Twitter is by using a largescale tactic – promoted trends. Trending topics on Twitter change all the time. Every user is able to see what is currently popular in their area. By clicking on a trend, you are able to browse through tweets that contain information relevant to each one. Promoting a trend is a way to encourage users to talk about your business. This type of advertising can bring awareness to your brand and create an association with your products. No matter which method you select, getting on a desktop to create these ads is going to be the easiest way to do so. While Twitter itself is very mobile friendly, you can do a lot more with Twitter Ads on the website version.

Tumblr

Tumblr is a platform that is used mostly by the younger generation. If Tumblr is a suitable platform for your business, creating a Tumblr page can definitely provide some benefits. First, you need to understand what Tumblr is used for before you can decide if it is a platform that will fit your business needs. If you have ever wanted to create a blog, then you will probably find Tumblr to be very useful. It is a comprehensive way to keep a blog that can either be for personal or business use. While there are not many businesses on the platform, Tumblr has been used successfully by some savvy entrepreneurs to grow their business and brand.

Tumblr is a way for anyone to be able to express opinions, post creative content, and promote products. You are given the chance to use HTML on Tumblr, which is a feature that sets it apart from the rest. Admittedly, it does take more time to learn Tumblr than any of the apps previously mentioned. This learning gap can be closed by viewing some simple tutorials, though. A fully customizable page gives you a way to really present your business in the best light possible.

Users like Tumblr because it can be used for just about anything with minimal censorship. A lot of other social media outlets heavily censor content and even ban users for posting what is considered "inappropriate." Tumblr is known for being very lax with their guidelines. Because it is less structured, having a vision for your brand is very important. If you don't have a vision or guidelines to follow, your Tumblr likely won't become successful. It can be easy for pages to be overlooked if they are not interesting and unique.

As a business on a mostly personal platform, you can't make your page too ad focused. Instead, keep the selling points to a minimum. Sharing information with your potential clients about how your product will fit their lifestyle is a good way to begin. In this case especially, authenticity is going to be important. People don't flock to Tumblr to find their next car dealership. They use Tumblr as a way of expression and as an outlet. Don't be afraid to create personal connections with those who follow you. Much like other forms of social media, you can like, re-post, comment, and follow on the platform.

Advertising on Tumblr allows you the option to create sponsored posts, just like most other social media platforms. You are given the analytics to carefully track your audience and the responses your posts receive. Selecting the right demographic is very important with Tumblr. Since it can be harder to find profiles, a little bit of research needs to be done regarding what users are most interested in. This can take quite a bit of trial and error, making it difficult for some brands to target the right audiences with their advertising efforts. This is why a lot of businesses don't care to create a page. However, if you take the time to master the platform, it can be a great resource.

If you want to go with a free advertising option, you can simply create informative posts and encourage people to repost them. A lot of luck is involved with this method, but you can use hashtags and enticing captions to pave the way. Most of the same etiquette is applicable here as it is on Instagram. Go for hashtags that are popular and create content that will catch the eye. Many users become annoyed by anything that is too formal on Instagram, so always check in with your analytics to see how your posts are performing.

LinkedIn

LinkedIn is a social media platform that is geared toward professionals. It was originally created to assist with employment opportunities, but it has become so much more. In order to create a business page, you must start by creating a personal page. This part takes some work as LinkedIn has standards for your personal page to meet in order to move on to the next step. Some of these include having the profile for at least 7 days, having a unique email address, and having plenty of connections (these are your friends on the platform). If you are able to meet the lengthy list of requirements, then you will qualify. Because it is geared toward professionals, LinkedIn likes to do this as a way of filtering content. If they know that you meet these requirements, then they know that your content is going to be up to par.

If you are willing to put in the effort to set up both of these pages, you will be granting your business some extra exposure. In addition to the regular social media advertising features (pay-per-click ads), you can use your business page as a way to form connections with other professionals. This is a great way to start collaborations and partnerships. LinkedIn is very much about reaching out to others. You can share informative articles, photos, and videos, and also direct message other users. These are the main components that you will experience.

If it is possible to set up a business page for your company, this is one way to build up your reputation in the industry. You might not qualify at first, but over time, it can be a goal that you can work toward. Being established is a connotation that comes along with having a business LinkedIn page. This shows that you are organized and dedicated to your company. While it might not be the most effective platform for advertising, it can still produce results.

If you plan on hiring in the future, LinkedIn has you covered. This is what the platform was originally designed for. It connects you with professionals that are interested in applying for different work positions. You are able to share the vision of your business along with explaining a bit of its back story. Customers aren't the only ones who like to hear this type of behind-the-scenes information. If someone is going to work for you, they should be aware of what exactly the brand represents.

Having a LinkedIn account is not essential, but it can prove to be helpful. While it is less customizable than most other platforms, its simplicity is what makes it effective for business owners. Keep in mind that not all business types are going to benefit from having one, and that is okay. It is up to you as the owner to decide if LinkedIn makes sense for what you do. Admittedly, the pay-per-click rates aren't the best out of the different platforms available. If you are looking for something more reasonable, you are better off starting with Instagram or Facebook.

How Many Pages Should a Business Have?

Learning about how many different social media platforms exist can leave a business owner wondering how many profiles should be created. Should you stick to just one? Should you aim to create a profile on every platform that seems like it will benefit the company? The choice is up to you, but there are a few things that you should consider when narrowing down your selection:

- **Realistic Time Expectations**: Remember, running a social media page does take some time and effort. If you don't hire someone to do it for you, then you are the one who is responsible for keeping your content consistent. While it doesn't take an absurd amount of time, you do need to make sure that you have a keen eye for detail. After doing your research on how to use a particular platform, you must make sure that your content is of top quality. After you begin your marketing campaign, you are going to need to do constant monitoring of the analytics to determine if it is a success. Operating your social media accounts should become a daily part of your work routine. If you have just one or two profiles to manage, this shouldn't be too difficult. However, if you have half a dozen different pages to monitor, this can become very time consuming.

- **Ease of Use**: Just because one platform is proven to be popular doesn't mean that it is going to be the most user-friendly. We all have different comfort levels when it comes to social media. Even the most experienced of users still have preferences. Using preference as a basis of your decision is perfectly acceptable. Go with the social media option that is going to work best for you personally. Social media should be relatively fun, so make sure that you are picking the platforms that work best for you.

- **Competitive Pricing**: While most of these social media platforms provide the same type of advertising services and resources, you might notice a price difference. Much like anything that you shop for, making your decision based on this price point is being business-savvy. Your budget likely only allows you a set amount to be spent on advertising, so make sure that you are distributing these funds in the smartest way possible.

- **Demographic Search**: Think about the audience that you want to appeal to. After using most social media and taking a look at the different niches, you will be able to get a feel for the type of demographic that it attracts. For example, LinkedIn contains more of a professional crowd while Facebook has users from all walks of life. This is not to say that one social media platform is better than another, but the demographics will impact the success of your marketing campaigns.

- **Customization Factors**: If you are looking for a creative outlet, you will need to select a suitable platform that allows for creativity. Not all of them are fully customizable. When you are a business that is known for a certain appearance or creative outlook, you will need to make sure that your social media accounts reflect this. Even if you do not opt to use HTML, making sure that you can stay "on brand" is a good indication if the platform is going to be a good fit for you. Not everyone cares about this, but a business that wants to remain cohesive should take it into consideration.

Chapter 8: How to Keep Momentum Going

Once your Instagram page is operational, the work does not stop there. A lot of businesses make the mistake of only going through the motions, creating an account, and becoming lazy with their posting schedule after using it for a few weeks. If you want to see continued growth, you are going to have to permanently dedicate some time each day to ensure that you are correctly managing your social media. Not only do you need to remain operational on the platform, but you must also remember to encourage your customers to interact with you on it. Some businesses forget that asking existing customers to follow an Instagram page can result in a wave of growth.

Spreading the Word

When it comes to letting people know about your brand's Instagram page, there isn't much to it other than telling them. Tell your customers to give you a follow and mention what kind of content you post. This would be a great time to mention exclusive discount offers, if you have any. Much like on the actual platform, you need to entice the audience. Give them a reason to want to follow your account. Keep the conversation minimal and casual. A simple mention of the account is good enough because you won't want your customers feeling pressured. Even though the platform is growing tremendously, not everyone has an Instagram account. In addition, not everyone likes to follow business accounts.

Make sure that you put a link to your Instagram on your website. You can install what is known as a "widget." This is a small icon that the customer can click on to be redirected to your Instagram page. If you choose, you can even display a preview of your Instagram profile directly onto your website. This is another very minimal technique that you can use to encourage your customers to follow your account. Sometimes, people are just curious. Maybe someone who wasn't planning on making a purchase decided to click on your Instagram widget; seeing a more in-depth look into your brand might lead to that person to change his or her mind.

Advertising social media accounts on business cards is another great way to let your customers know that you have them. Since a business card has very minimal space, you probably won't want to add text that asks a person to follow your account. Instead, consider just placing the Instagram logo near the bottom, alongside your other social media logos. This is a smart way to subliminally mention to your customers that they should add you on social media. As long as your username is true to your brand, there should be no trouble with finding your account. If you do have the room, you can put your username next to the logo just to be sure.

A business that displays the desire to stay current is one that consumers are often going to be willing to engage with. Having an Instagram account for your business is a sign that you are in touch with what is current and modern. While you don't need to have the trendiest account, people do appreciate when you take the time to adapt your business to the current culture. It is amazing how fast this type of technology has grown, allowing for connectivity in ways that weren't possible mere years ago.

Social Media Manager

If you feel that the commitment is going to be too time consuming, you can hire someone to help you run your social media accounts. This position is known as a social media manager, and it is very popular with businesses nowadays to hire one. There should be no stigma attached. If you feel that you are too busy, it makes sense that you would want to ask for help. This person will be assigned to your account and given instructions on your vision. When you have your initial conversation, you can explain your backstory and mission. If you want to have even more of a say in what happens on the account, you can provide the content that is to be posted each week.

No matter what the arrangement is, your social media manager is there to make your experience easier. Whether you want a little help or a complete take over, this is to be discussed before you hire someone. Make sure that you take a look at personal references and other businesses who utilize the service. Because you are going to have to give this person access to your account, it should be someone who is trustworthy and has a good reputation.

If possible, you can reach out to other businesses who use the social media manager. Ask about how easy the person is to work with. Since you are going to be speaking a lot, you will want to make sure that you are hiring someone with a positive mindset. Getting honest opinions from the source will help you to make the best decision for your company. As mentioned, hiring someone to do this job is very common in today's business landscape, so you'll likely find plenty of different social media managers out there to choose from.

Change Your Approach

Because Instagram is ever-changing, you can model your approach in the same way. If you have been posting on a certain schedule, try changing it up. Remember, it is a good idea to post on Instagram frequently. If you have been posting 3 times each week, try switching to 4 or 5. A small change like this might be enough to reset your algorithm and push your posts to the top of news feeds. While there is no clear-cut way for the average person to learn all of Instagram's patterns, it does help to try changing things up to see if anything new happens.

The same can be said for the way that you post captions and hashtags. Maybe you have been loading each post with a dozen tags; try instead to only include 3-4. Every change that you make on social media is going to be trial and error. None of these minor changes should result in any dramatically negative outcomes, but you do need to make some alterations if you find that your social media growth has been stagnant lately.

Perhaps you need to start an ad campaign. Instead of another campaign that simply advertises who you are, try to offer your customers something that they need. If it is possible, hold a sale and make it Instagram exclusive. Customers appreciate getting special treatment, and a sale of this category feels as such. You can also start a referral program; if a customer brings you another sale, they can obtain a personal discount code. There are plenty of ways to revamp your marketing campaigns with some creativity and careful planning.

Starting a new theme for your feed is also a great way to update your content that takes very minimal effort. Pick a different color scheme and give your followers some variety. While it isn't necessary to have a theme in the first place, it does give your feed a more professional look. Posts that are visually appealing are more likely to result in the individual reading your caption. Make sure that you post the highest quality images to accompany captions that are important to read.

Dedicated Live Streams

If possible, try to go live on your account each week. You can do anything from hosting a Q&A to showing people what a day at your company looks like. Users like to view live streams because it gives them the ability to satisfy curiosity without making a commitment. They will have the chance to ask questions or make comments at will. Going live is always a great way to encourage people to be proactive about interacting. It does take a certain comfort level to be able to go live in front of the camera. If you or your staff aren't comfortable with this, you can turn the focus onto your product(s) instead.

It is okay if you need to plan out a draft of what points you would like to talk about during the live stream. While you don't want to sound scripted, sometimes it can be beneficial to have a loose idea of topics rather than just improvising the entire thing. This is entirely up to your own discretion and comfort level. A live stream should be fun for both you and the viewers. Think about what you would most like to see during a live stream.

Live streaming is very much a newer form of technology that is being utilized by businesses. It is no longer exclusive to gamers and those in the beauty industry who do tutorials. A live stream can be done on just about anything, as long as you have an idea of what you'd like to talk about. The conversation can really begin to flow if you get enough interactive viewers involved. If held on a regular basis, these people will begin to look forward to your company's live streams.

Geotagging Locations

Create a geotag for your business. This is something that you can tag as a location on all of your posts. Your geotag will include your business name and address (when clicked on). If you have a physical location, this is a great feature to add to your posts that will apply no matter what you post. If a customer is considering visiting your store, clicking on the geotag will provide them with the location address. Although this isn't the only place that you can feature your business address, it is an additional way to answer a question before a customer needs to ask.

People like being able to be self-reliant. If your location is easy to find, someone will be more likely to visit and make a purchase. This does have a lot to do with the recent development of technology. Consumers prefer not to write emails and make phone calls. They like being able to review information independently before making their decisions. Social media can be a hub of information, able to be browsed by just about anyone. Giving your clients as much information as possible is a way to build up your reputation. You want to come across as easy to work with and efficient.

Geotagging can also be utilized when you are holding any type of event. By tagging the location in your post and listing the date and time in the content, your customer will have all of the relevant information at their fingertips. With Instagram, this type of communication is easily possible. Also, it comes at no cost to you. If you were to advertise an event in a more traditional way, you would have to pay for content to be created for you and then it would still be up to you to distribute it.

Your Interactions

There is a duality to Instagram; users can interact with you and you can also interact with others. It is important to show a mutual reciprocation of interaction with the people that you follow. You do not necessarily have to give a like for every single like that you get, but it is a nice thing to return some of them. This shows that you are an active user on the platform and that your followers will benefit from having you on their friends list. Liking, commenting, and sharing is not only appropriate but it is encouraged for a business account. Some business owners forget that this is the way that Instagram works; what you put out; you will likely get in return.

Once you get into the habit of interacting with others, you will find it very easy to do. Instagram is meant to be a way to discover and explore, not to be bogged down with sales pitches left and right. Logging on a few times a day can break up the amount of time that you have to spend focused on social media, if you feel that you cannot dedicate enough time to it. To many, browsing on Instagram is just a part of their daily routine. This same principle can apply to businesses that wish to grow as well. Get into the habit of posting and interacting. You might form some lasting connections and even opportunities for collaborations.

Because this is not your personal social media page, you do need to make sure that you are appropriate with what you say and do. You wouldn't want people to take a look at your like history and discover that you liked an influx of inappropriate content. It is best to keep your likes and comments relevant to your business in some way. Remember that your followers are able to see what you are liking, so keep that in mind any time you decide to interact with others on the app.

What you like will impact your algorithm. If you continue liking posts that fit within your niche, Instagram will show you more users that fit these parameters. Liking a lot of posts is a sure way to boost your posts in the algorithm. This is where the time and effort come in to maintaining an Instagram account. Some users spend up to hours a day devoting their time to interacting with other users' posts. Make sure that you do set aside a realistic amount of time to do this with your own followers. Staying active in this way will help you remain relevant on other's timelines.

Make sure that you don't act as a spammer would. This is the type of account that likes just about anything in a short amount of time, leaving comments on content that are not relevant. This can actually have a negative effect and cause you to be blacklisted. Instagram does its best to keep spam off of the platform. Keep what you say and do genuine. This will prevent users from becoming annoyed at your interactions. Instagram is very much like a give and take kind of app. You will begin to learn the patterns of its algorithm by using Instagram on a regular basis.

Conclusion

Thanks again for taking the time to read this book!

You should now have a good understanding of Instagram, how the platform works, and have a plethora of new ways to grow your brand and business.

The next step is to implement some of the strategies you have learned about in this book, remembering to constantly track your results, and test which strategies work best for you. With consistent effort, Instagram can prove to be an essential part of your business growth and success!

www.ingramcontent.com/pod-product-compliance
Lightning Source LLC
LaVergne TN
LVHW011718060526
838200LV00051B/2936